The Quiet Heart

The Quiet Heart

Martyn Lloyd-Jones

CROSSWAY BOOKS
Leicester

© Elizabeth Catherwood and Ann Desmond 1995

First edition 1995

This edition published by arrangement with
Servant Publications,
PO Box 8617,
Ann Arbor, Michigan, 48107

British Library Cataloguing in Publication Data
A catalogue record for this book is available from the British
Library.

ISBN 1-86584-117-0

Printed in Great Britain for Crossway Books,
38 De Montfort Street, Leicester, LE1 7GP,
by Cox & Wyman Ltd, Reading, Berkshire.

Contents

❧

Foreword

∾

OUR FATHER, MARTYN LLOYD-JONES (1899-1981), preached these sermons in 1951 in Westminster Chapel in London. These were difficult times for the people of Britain—indeed for all the Western world. The Second World War was not long over, with all the economic, political, national, and personal problems it had left in its wake. But then there was also the menace of the Cold War, with the nuclear threat which hung over both sides. There was not the same euphoria as there had been after the First World War; people were anxious and fearful.

So it was in this atmosphere that our father preached this short series of sermons. They were intended to comfort, strengthen, and build up Christians in their "most holy faith" and to bring unbelievers to a knowledge of the only way in which men and women can face such matters of life and death. He sought to show that these familiar words were not only relevant in funerals but applied to all facets of our lives, and the way in which he handled these words was very characteristic of his ministry. He did not use them as a kind of soothing refrain which would lull our fears to rest. Rather, he went through them carefully, showing that the way to deal with our fears was first to confront them and recognise them and then to realise that the answer to them was only to be found in the great and unchanging truths of the Christian Gospel.

So he shows what these are: belief in God, belief in Jesus Christ and His work; the certainty of His promise that He will take us safely to His Father's house, and so on. These are foundational doctrines but he does not deal with them clinically. Throughout we are reminded of the love which brought it all to pass.

He once described preaching as "logic on fire," and this is very evident in these sermons. They are, perhaps, briefer in their exposition than, for example, his later great series on Romans and Ephesians, but the truths and the spirit are the same.

Towards the end of his life, when he was very weak, he experienced for himself these things that he had preached earlier. One evening his doctor said to him, "I don't like to see you weary and worn and sad like this."

"No!" came back the whispered answer, "Not sad!" He pointed us in the family to the great verses in 2 Corinthians 4:16-18:

For which cause we faint not; but though our outward man perish, yet the inward man is renewed day by day. For our light affliction, which is but for a moment, worketh for us a far more exceeding and eternal weight of glory; While we look not at the things which are seen, but at the things which are not seen: for the things which are seen are temporal; but the things which are not seen are eternal.

He also asked us not to pray for healing. "Don't," he said, "try to hold me back from the glory." He was ill for many months, but the great truths of John 14 held him fast. He knew that the Saviour, whom he had served so faithfully for so many years, had prepared a place for him. He knew the quiet heart, the stillness of the soul, of which these sermons speak.

Elizabeth Catherwood
Ann Desmond
September 9, 1994

PART I
We Must Believe

✺

"Let not your heart be troubled:
ye believe in God,
believe also in me."
John 14:1

ONE

"Let Not Your Heart Be Troubled"

Let not your heart be troubled:
ye believe in God, believe also in me.
John 14:1

A S WE COME TO CONSIDER this great passage together, I think that most commentators agree that a better way of putting it is: "Let not your heart be troubled, believe in God, believe also in me." In other words, it is probably right to say that it is the imperative that we have in both cases.

However these words are probably familiar to most of us; indeed they are, perhaps, some of the most familiar and tender words ever uttered by our Lord and Saviour Jesus Christ. They are words, therefore, which we often tend to take without really facing them and their real meaning, and without analyzing them as we should. It is to me a real tragedy that so often we rob ourselves of the real message of some of the most glorious statements in Scripture simply because we regard them as literature. We are content with some

13

general effect or influence that they may produce upon us, instead of taking the trouble to arrive at their exact meaning and their precise import.

Now that, I think, is very true of these words, words that may be most familiar to us in funerals. They are words of comfort and consolation, which we tend, therefore, to think of far too often as some kind of beautiful music or some wonderful diction. So we never get any further, almost feeling at times that it is a sacrilege to analyse something which is so beautiful.

> "Let not your heart be troubled: ye believe in God, believe also in me. In my Father's house are many mansions: if it were not so, I would have told you. I go to prepare a place for you. And if I go and pre-pare a place for you, I will come again, and receive you unto myself; that where I am, there ye may be also.... Peace I leave with you, my peace I give unto you.... Let not your heart be troubled, neither let it be afraid."
>
> **John 14:1-3, 27**

We have heard those words many times, but I wonder what would happen if we suddenly had to sit down with paper in front of us and face a question like this: "State the doctrine contained in those familiar words— what exactly do they say?" Have these words, I wonder, come to us merely in that general manner, that kind of general consolation, which, as I say, can be done equally well by beautiful music or by any beautiful thoughts or passages of literature? Or have we derived comfort and consolation from them because we have realised the doctrine that they are announcing?

Our Lord's whole purpose in uttering these words was that He might instruct His disciples and help them, by bringing them to a deeper knowledge and understanding of truth. He was addressing their minds primarily and the way in which He came to do so is of significance and importance. He had just been telling these men, who had now accompanied Him for about three years, that He was about to leave them. He was still young, in His early thirties, and, to their astonishment and utter chagrin, He announced that He was going to leave them. "Now," He said, "is the Son of man glorified, and God is glorified in him…. Little children, yet a little while I am with you. Ye shall seek me: and as I said unto the Jews, Whither I go, ye cannot come; so now I say to you" (Jn 13:31, 33). But He realised at once that this information had upset these disciples and had made them unhappy and disconsolate. Their hearts had become troubled, they were ill at ease and they had lost their peace because they were suddenly confronted by a problem.

Now we need not go into details here as to why the disciples felt this so acutely; that has its interest and its importance, but we need not stay with it. It might very well have been due to the fact that they had become overdependent upon Him; they had never met anybody like Him before. They had been ordinary men living ordinary lives in this world, having their ups and downs and problems, but suddenly they had met Him and had been called by Him to follow Him and keep Him company in a very special way, and it had been a marvellous and thrilling experience. His very personality was something quite apart and unique, they had never seen anybody like this before. There was something in His very person; to look into His eyes meant something that they had never known.

Then it was amazing to hear His extraordinary teaching, His gracious words, His knowledge, His understanding; to see Him performing miracles, cleansing the leper, making the lame to walk, giving sight to the blind, even raising the dead; and thus, imperceptibly, they had become entirely dependent upon Him. I suppose the temptation in such a situation was that they would not stop to think, they just relied utterly upon Him; and then, suddenly, He announced that He was going away, and at once they were filled with a sense of alarm and concern. Did that mean that they would have to go back to where they were before; did it mean a reversion to their hopeless kind of life? "How can we do without Him?" they thought. "If He is going, then we are finished, we are undone." And our Lord recognised that they were thinking all this.

Or it may have been that they had recognised in Him, rather vaguely and dimly yet surely, the Messiah who was expected. They had their Jewish notions as to what the Messiah was to be and about the kingdom He was to establish and it was very largely political. They had been troubled because He had not set Himself up as king; some had tried to force Him to do so. They had decided to wait upon Him, feeling that, at some point not far removed, he would just declare Himself. He would set Himself up as king, make a great attack upon the Romans, and so rid them of the Roman tyranny and set up a wonderful kingdom. But here He was, announcing that He was going away! He had done nothing about bringing in the kingdom, so they were unhappy and had a feeling that they had been misled and somewhat deluded; He was not what they thought He was going to be.

Well, they no doubt had many such thoughts, but the important thing is that our Lord sensed all this in them. He saw that they had become disturbed and unhappy and that, above all, their trouble was in their hearts. Their hearts were "troubled," and so, in a very characteristic manner, He dealt with their troubles and administered to them this glorious word of consolation.

There is also one other preliminary remark that I must make at this point; it is vital that we should remember at what time in His life our Lord did this. It was on the very eve of the Cross. He knew what was coming; He had been earlier on the Mount of Transfiguration, and there Moses and Elijah had spoken to Him concerning "his decease which he should accomplish at Jerusalem" (Lk 9:31). He knew what was going to be involved on the Cross; He knew He was being made sin for mankind; He knew that when God would lay on Him the sins of us all, it would mean a terrible moment of separation from the face of God. He knew all that and, as He said later on in the Garden of Gethsemane, His soul was "exceeding sorrowful" (Mt 26:38), yet He nevertheless turned aside to comfort these unhappy followers of His. He was more concerned about their unhappiness than His own immediate problem, and thus we have this wonderful view, that on the very eve of the Cross, our Lord gave Himself freely in comfort and consolation to others.

> B*earing in His own body the sins of the world, He had sufficient compassion and love and sympathy and understanding to turn to the wretched man who was there being crucified with Him.* ✎

How typical and characteristic of Him! He did the same thing on the Cross itself, you remember—even after they had driven the cruel nails into His hands and His feet. There dying upon the Cross, He had time to spare and to speak to that thief, dying by His side. Bearing in His own body the sins of the world, He had sufficient compassion and love and sympathy and understanding to turn to the wretched man who was there being crucified with Him.

Now I emphasise all this at the beginning because, whatever else we may or may not learn as we consider this passage, let us realise that the one about whom we are speaking, the one about whom we are concerned, is one like that. That is the Jesus, the Saviour, the Lord Jesus Christ whom we preach; He is the centre of this New Testament message and Gospel. He is the one who, though He is the Son of God Himself, is ready and willing and able to meet us exactly where we are. He even takes the trouble to read our minds and thoughts in order to answer our questions before we have ever put them and He gives us consolation before we have ever given expression to our need and unhappiness.

So as He said this to the disciples, He says it, of course, once and for ever, to all others who at any time or in any age, or in any place know this same condition of the troubled heart. Here in these three chapters, chapters 14, 15 and 16 of John's Gospel, we have our Lord administering this final comfort and consolation to all who feel overwhelmed and bewildered by the problems of life and of existence.

I suppose that in many ways it can truthfully be said that the greatest need of men and women in this world is the need of what is called "the quiet heart," a heart at leisure from itself.

> The greatest need of men and women in this world is the need of what is called "the quiet heart." ∾

Is that not, in the last analysis, the thing for which we are all looking? You can if you like call it peace; that means exactly the same thing, peace of mind and peace of heart, tranquillity. We are all restless, we are all disturbed. There is this unhappiness in us and it is produced by many different causes.

One thing that causes all our hearts to be restless

and disturbed, one thing that robs everybody of peace, is the very thought of death. This is a great and certain fact; in the words of the woman of Tekoah, "For we must needs die, and are as water spilt on the ground, which cannot be gathered up again" (2 Sm 14:14). It is a most disturbing, a most troubling thought. The author of the epistle to the Hebrews says that, until we become Christians, we are all in life-long bondage "through fear of death" (Heb 2:15). Shakespeare, who knew the human heart, gives these words to Hamlet: "The dread of something after death—the undiscovered country, from whose bourne no traveller returns..."

"Conscience," he adds, "doth make cowards of us all." Yes, we do this and that, but thought of that "undiscovered country" upsets everything; that is the trouble and that is a cause of the restless unquiet heart.

Then, there are also the problems that are incidental to life in this world, life and its almost inevitable ills, these things, which come sooner or later: illness, accident, disappointment, financial loss, trouble in business, the serious illness of a child or a loved one, the death of somebody else; these are the things that come and that test us all and we cannot avoid them. We all want to make our plans for life and living. When we think we have made our perfect plans, something suddenly happens and our whole world begins to shake and to quake. There are certain ills which simply cannot be avoided; things that are bound to happen, the tragedies of life.

And all this, of course, is quite apart from the fact of the particular problems of this twentieth century. Every age of mankind has been subject to the things which I have mentioned, but we in this century, on top of these things, have this uncertain world in which we are living, with all the possibility of wars and all these other threats. The supreme problem is that of trying to face these things and to achieve a quiet heart. I think that any analysis of modern literature and of the conduct of the vast majority of people will indicate very clearly that what people are doing is trying to achieve peace in some shape or form.

> W*e need to determine what is really likely to give us this quiet heart.* ∾

We need to determine what is really likely to give us this quiet heart. For we must start by being realistic and by saying that it is not only the Christian Gospel that offers us freedom from the troubled heart. There are many ways in which we are exhorted to try to find this, so I must start with the negative. I must deal with the false before I can come to the true, because there are men and women who are holding on to these things and then, because they do not find satisfaction, they come and listen to the Gospel. The claim of the Gospel is not only that it can give us a quiet heart, but also that nothing else can do it.

Of course people do not like that sort of claim today; they say that it is "intolerant." We are living in

22

days when people are always saying, "We want a world conference of all the religions, so let us all get together and pick out the best in each." But you cannot do that with the Gospel of Jesus Christ; it is exclusive and its challenge is that the Gospel, and it alone, can truly give us peace.

Now let me substantiate that by reminding you of some of the other ways in which it is suggested we can find this. One is that we should refuse to think. We must put that first because it is the commonest. This is a quite definite philosophy; people say increasingly that if you are foolish enough to think in this world, then it is not surprising that you are unhappy, and, in a sense, you deserve to be so. They say that the whole trouble with men and women is that they will persist in thinking; if only they had the sense to stop doing that and to be just like the animals and go back to nature and live the animal life, all would be well. That was the philosophy of D.H. Lawrence, who said that man has over-developed the higher part of his brain but that if only he would revert to the lower type of life, he would be much happier. There are many who say that, though not in such a philosophical way. "If you want to be happy," they say, "just get away from your troubles." So you fill up the agenda of your life as much as you can with meeting other people, going to entertainments and all these other things—in other words, escapism.

Then another way in which we are told that we can achieve the quiet heart is that we should espouse and adopt the philosophy of what is called *optimism*, and it is astounding that there are still many who follow this philosophy. It takes many shapes and forms. Some still cling tenaciously to their belief in an inevitable kind of evolution to a better life. They say that the whole of mankind is gradually evolving to a higher state and a more perfect condition in which our troubles and problems will be left behind; and they still believe that in spite of all that has happened in the past one hundred years! There are others who do not put it exactly like that, but their optimism just consists in saying, "It is all right; there are these temporary setbacks, but," they say, "things are going to be better." This happened before the Second World War; such people were quite sure, up to the last minute, that Hitler would see wisdom. This is belief in optimism for the sake of being optimistic. People are proud of this; they go on looking at the bright side of things, and believe it is their duty to be always smiling, come what may. There are many trying to achieve the quiet heart in that way.

Then, going up the scale a little, we come to the next which is what I would call the philosophy of fatalism. I think that this is becoming increasingly common. To put it in its simplest form, it says, "What is to be will be; and all the thinking, and all the worrying and all the calculating in the world cannot affect it. Of course, the trouble with people is that they will persist in thinking, but if only they saw that to do that is to exaggerate the trouble, they would stop thinking and making themselves unhappy. It is because they go to meet their troubles and anticipate them that they are so troubled. But everything seems to be rigidly fixed by a fatalistic principle; therefore do not think, wait until things do happen and, at any rate, you will have a kind of temporary peace and an assuaging of your trouble." There are many who pacify themselves and think they can get true peace that way.

Then the next is what I would call the psychological method. This is slightly different because it attempts a kind of positive and active treatment of us and of our minds. It is just a device to train us to play tricks with our own thoughts and hearts; in a sense, it is not interested in our problems, it is interested in our reaction to those problems. The psychologist is one who is concerned with giving us peace of mind; that is his objective. The different types of psychological treatment all say the same thing to us, "Why worry?" They try to show us, in various ways, the folly of worrying. They tell us to try to think of beautiful and pleasant things; they say that we must deliberately subjugate our thoughts and project them on to other things and so on. So when people become agitated, they rush to a psychologist.

Then, still going up the scale, the next thing is the definite adopting of a kind of attitude of resignation or of stoicism. Or, as they seem to prefer to call it today, "the scientific attitude," or "the psychological calm." There are many people who talk about this attitude. They say the one thing we must watch is our feelings. Our trouble is that we all tend to be controlled by our feelings, and if our feelings take over, then we become agitated and unhappy. So the solution to that, they say, is the adoption of this particular teaching. We must stand back and have a psychological calm, we must become scientists. There is nothing new about all that; the Stoics did it all long ago; that was the very essence of their philosophy, that you must always keep a careful curb upon your feelings and emotions, otherwise they will cripple you. So you must take yourself in hand and control your emotions and you must go on and say to yourself, "Now I must be objective, I must be scientific, I must not let myself be immersed in these things."

And that brings me to the last philosophy and that is the one which is provided by cults and other religions like Christian Science, which deliberately set out to give people freedom from trouble and worry, a kind of perfect calm in spite of everything. There are other cults which try to do the same thing. I refer to "the cults and other religions" because there is a remarkable increase in the number of such religions today, chiefly coming from the East, which offer this escape from trouble and the way to a quiet heart. There is a new interest in Buddhism and in Hinduism and things of that kind. (It is very interesting to notice that it is some of the men who used to call themselves intellectuals who are turning to Buddhism and to these Eastern religions and various forms of mysticism. They have tried to face their problems and they have failed. So they have come to the conclusion that their only salvation is in mysticism, going into the heart of the universe, losing themselves in the spirit that is at the back of everything.) And there are many who are seeking this quiet heart, and deliverance from their troubles, in that way.

I am always so sorry for the "bright young things...." The actual truth about them is that they are so afraid of life that they dare not think about it. ❧

Now obviously we cannot deal with all these things now, but I am concerned to say that there are certain general comments that can be made about them all. It seems to me, first, that they are, all of them in the last analysis, pessimistic and hopeless. To refuse to think is to be profoundly pessimistic; that is why I am always so sorry for the "bright young things," the people who live for pleasure and say, "How happy we are by contrast with you miserable Christians!" But the actual truth about them is that they are so afraid of life that they dare not think about it. That is the profoundest pessimism that I know.

It is exactly the same with this pathetic optimism that refuses to face the facts that are here confronting us in this twentieth century. There is no evidence that man as man is progressing and evolving. It is the same with fatalism, which is utterly hopeless. It says, "What is the use of anything? Things are just going to happen, therefore do nothing about them and do not even think about them."

It is the same also with resignation; resignation says, "Things are going to be like this, so I have just got to put up with them somehow"—that again is hopelessness. Psychology, as I have said, does not even face the problem; it plays tricks with itself. It is like whistling in the dark; and the same applies to the cults and these various other religions. You may have to be reincarnated many times, but your hope is that you eventually become merged into the universe—and that too, is profound pessimism. So all these views, at their very best and highest, are devised just to help us to get through, they simply help us to postpone our problems, they do not solve them; and none of them can give us real joy or satisfaction.

But I suppose the greatest criticism of them is that they, all of them in a sense, leave the problem to me. How true this is of the Eastern religions! You will find that they leave it to you; you will have to go through terrible ordeals, you will have to discipline your body, mind, and every part of yourself. They will ask you to deliver yourself in some shape or form, and thus they leave us with the problem. To me it is very significant that the people who are turning to Buddhism are, as we have said, the so-called "intellectuals." You have to be an intellectual before you can go in for such things because they leave it to you, and it takes a lot of thinking time to employ these methods of attaining peace. They have nothing whatever to give to the ordinary person. They have nothing to give those who are so hardworked with their jobs, their families, their homes and various other things that they cannot read these wonderful philosophical ideas. Ordinary people have no time to go through these long processes of discipline and prayer. Eastern religions have nothing to give such people.

S o all these views... simply help us to *postpone our problems, they do not solve them; and none of them can give us real joy....* ✑

Then the trouble I find with psychology is that it is simply an attempt to give you quiet nerves, instead of giving you a quiet heart. I want to be fair to psychology. It can give us, up to a point, quiet nerves, but that is not what we need, we need a quiet heart. Thank God for something that, as far as it goes, can give us quiet nerves, but do you want to be at rest on the surface or do you want to be at rest in the very depths and vitals of your being? And it is at that point that the Gospel claims that it, and it alone, can meet and satisfy our deepest need, and here we are told exactly how it does it.

I am simply introducing this subject now; we shall go on to consider it in detail, but let me just give you an outline of it. Here is something authoritative, something from Someone who has given us the truth from the dawn of history. Here is something that worked in these particular disciples to whom He was speaking. Here were men who, having listened to this Gospel and having proved it in their lives, were able to face the whole might and tyranny of the Roman Empire, with all its cruel persecutions; who came through more than conquerors, triumphing and rejoicing—read the great story of the apostles, and the martyrs, and the first confessors. It has worked and it continues to work.

There are other certain general statements which we

must make. What seems to me to be so entirely different about the Gospel, at the very beginning, is that it always faces facts, it is always realistic, it never conceals anything. You read these chapters of John's Gospel and you will find that our Lord brought these men face to face with the very worst, whereas all the other teachings and philosophies try to hide the worst from me. My heart will not be really quiet until I have been told the very worst and faced it, and then I can surmount it. I do not believe in a teaching that simply plays tricks with me. I have no use for a philosophy that tells me that there is no such thing as matter; and because of that there can be no pain and therefore I have not got pain—when I know there is pain. I know it may work psychologically; it may drug me for a time, I believe the lie and am relieved, but I do not merely want to be relieved of my pain, I want the disease to be faced and tackled.

The Gospel commends itself to me because of its truth, because it does not just say, "Well now let's forget our troubles and think of something beautiful." It says, "In the world ye shall have tribulation" (Jn 16:33); it says that in a world like this, dominated by Satan, there will be "wars and rumours of wars" (Mt 24:6); it is psychology and not the Gospel which just tries to make us forget our troubles for the time being. The Gospel of Jesus Christ always, therefore, of necessity, annoys certain people; people who think that a place of worship is just a place where you listen to beautiful things and, therefore, while you are sitting there you forget your problems and the problems of the world—these people are certain to be annoyed.

> *Our Lord brought these men face to face with the very worst [about themselves], whereas all the other teachings and philosophies try to hide the worst.* ❧

No, the Gospel confronts us with facts; it is all based upon a person; it is based upon certain things that happened historically. It comes and tells me, "Let not your heart be troubled." But it comes in the light of Gethsemane and the trial and the cruel crucifixion upon the Cross, the broken body, the burial, the utter hopelessness and despair. Then, and only then, it goes on to tell me of the Resurrection and the glory of the Ascension and the sending of the Holy Spirit, and that puts me in an entirely different position. It has taken me through the facts, through the tunnel of darkness to the dawn that lights the other end.

Moreover, it commends itself to me because it gives me an explanation and satisfies my mind. The Gospel has given this philosophy of history; it not only gives me the facts, it explains them, it puts them into a coherent whole. There is a great view of life in the Bible—we shall deal with that later. I am not finally helped by being told, for example, "It is all right, do not think about it, you will die and come back in some other form. You may go through a series of these incarnations and you will finally get lost in the vast universe." I do not believe that the whole trouble is my physical flesh, I know that the trouble is in my spirit. So I must have something that satisfies my mind. I want to face life; I want an explanation of why it is in the position that it is and I have the explanation here and only here.

I *do not believe that the whole trouble is my physical flesh, I know that the trouble is in my spirit.* ❧

And the thing that commends itself most of all to me is that it does not leave it all to me but it links all to the power of God. "Let not your heart be troubled"— why? "Believe in God, believe also in me," says Christ; "trust me." I have mentioned those who spend long weary hours in all the details of a busy everyday life; they cannot follow the "mystic way"; what have I to offer them? If I have not a Gospel that can give them a quiet heart, I have no Gospel worthy of the name. But thank God I do have a Gospel for them. I have a Gospel which tells them that the one who walked through this world and triumphed over it, even over death and the grave itself, has said this: "At that day ye shall know that I am in my Father, and ye in me, and I in you" (Jn 14:20), so that into their unutterable weakness comes the might and the power of the Son of God, who has vanquished death and the grave, and against Him nothing and no one can finally stand.

"Let not your heart be troubled:... believe in God."
Yes—the God of the Old Testament, the God of the
promises, the God of the covenants, the God of whom
it is said, "When my father and my mother forsake me,
then the Lord will take me up" (Ps 27:10). This is the
same God who has told mankind from the beginning
that His desire was to bless them, and to give them
peace and joy, and to have them as His children. Trust
Him; yes, but so often that is the difficulty, is it not? It
is all here in John 14. Philip, one of the disciples, said
to our Lord in effect, "If only we knew the Father, it
would suffice us, but the difficulty is knowing that
God in heaven is our Father." And our Lord's reply is,
"Have I been so long time with you, and yet hast thou
not known me, Philip?" (vv. 8-9). "Believe in God,
believe also in me," He says; "because without believing in me you will never really know the Father."

Thomas, too, had a problem: "We don't know this
way you are talking about," he said; and our Lord's
great answer to him was, "I am the way, the truth, and
the life: no man cometh unto the Father, but by me"
(vv. 5-6). And speaking about prayer—and how often
we find difficulty in this—He said, "It is all right, I am
going to be with the Father; if ye shall ask any thing in
my name, I will do it" (v. 14).

But then we say, "We are so weak, how can we go
through with it in a world like this?" He says, "It is all
right, I will not leave you comfortless" (v. 18), which
translated means, I will not leave you orphans, I will
"give you another Comforter" (v. 16), the blessed doc-

trine of the gift of the Holy Spirit. He comes and dwells within us and reveals and explains things, and energises and empowers and enables us.

> T *he Holy Spirit dwells within us and reveals and explains things, and energises and empowers and enables us.* ∾

It is all here in John's Gospel. But let me summarise it all that you may be encouraged; there has been one in this world called Jesus of Nazareth and it is He who says to you, "Let not your heart be troubled:... believe in me," which means, "Come to me, tell me your troubles, tell me all about that difficulty about God, the difficulty of prayer, the difficulty about your weak will and failure."

I do not care what it is; anything that makes you restless and ill at ease—it may be the possibility of war, it may be illness, it may be business troubles, it may be your own weakness morally in the realm of the will— whatever it is, whatever is troubling and making you unhappy, go to Him about it. He is the one who has so loved you as to die for you. He said, "Come unto me, all ye that labour and are heavy laden, and I will give you rest" (Mt 11:28). There is no need for you to be unhappy and restless. Believe in God, believe in the Son of God, the Lord Jesus Christ who came on earth to deliver you from that very thing and who has removed every barrier between you and God and who can give you rest and peace, here and now.

TWO

"Believe in God"

~

Thus saith the Lord the King of Israel,
and his redeemer the Lord of hosts; "I am the first,
and I am the last; and beside me there is no God."
Isaiah 44:6

WE HAVE BEEN CONSIDERING TOGETHER why it
was that our Lord spoke the words recorded in
John 14:1, "Let not your heart be troubled:... believe
in God, believe also in me." He spoke them primarily,
you remember, in order to comfort His disciples to
whom He had just made the announcement that He
was going to leave them. They were disappointed and
they were unhappy and they were afraid as they
thought of the future. So it was to deal with this that
our Lord spoke as He did and they are not only words
of comfort and consolation to those to whom they
were first spoken, but they have a message which is as
true today in this modern world of ours as it was then.
Furthermore, as I have been emphasising, it is a tried
method, something that worked in these very disciples.
You will recall that the effect of the most violent persecution upon them was just to make them meet

together in a prayer meeting, to thank God that they had been accounted worthy to suffer for His name's sake.

So, in the light of that, we have begun to discuss the whole question of how it is that we may obtain a quiet heart. We have considered some of the false methods that are suggested to us and we have realised that they do not meet the problem at all. So, having begun to look at our Lord's method, we now come to consider a little more in detail what this method is; and here He summarises it all in this one statement. "Let not your heart be troubled," He says. But how are we to avoid that?—and the answer is: "Believe in God, believe also in me."

The first thing, then, is to believe in God. ∾

The first thing, then, is to believe in God. This is always the starting point, the key to the understanding of the biblical method of giving to mankind the quiet heart. It can never be said too frequently that the Bible is not concerned primarily to give us a quiet heart; its interest is something else. Its primary concern is something that is infinitely more important, and unless we understand its purpose and understand that it is of the very essence of what we may call the biblical method, then we shall go hopelessly astray. The trouble with us is that we always tend to aim at these things directly; we always look for some immediate consolation, some immediate comfort.

Of course, this is true of us in every realm and department. I always feel that this can be best illustrated by using the physical analogy. A man who is taken ill is generally not interested in his disease as such; what he is interested in is, of course, the suffering which he has to endure because of the illness. He may have a pain, or he may be short of breath or something else, but the interest of the patient is invariably in his symptoms. What he wants is something to relieve them. I admit that this is perfectly natural, and there is nothing wrong in desiring to be free from pain; there is no merit in suffering it. But I must emphasise here that the Bible teaches us that we must not only be concerned with the relief of the pain.

> A*nything which merely gives us relief from the unpleasant symptoms... is not enough.... what we should always be interested in, in every realm, is health.*

A man who sins suffers remorse; he has an agony of mind and the one thing he wants is to get rid of that agony. But what he really needs is much more than immediate comfort. Anything which merely gives us relief from the unpleasant symptoms of our disease or from our agony of mind is not enough. In fact, it is doing us a very grave disservice; for what we should always be interested in, in every realm, is health. That is the thing to aim at; not merely an absence of trouble but the positive condition of health.

Now it is at that point that we come across what is the great differentiating and characteristic feature of the Bible and its method. You see, nearly all these other methods that are being offered to us today are simply concerned to give us immediate relief from pain. They are all drugs in some shape or form, they have just that one interest—to relieve us. And many people come to God and to God's house in that kind of way, expecting to have some temporary relief of pain, something that can make them happy. But the Bible teaches us always that happiness and joy and peace, and the absence of pain and trouble, are always by-products; they are always the result of something else. They are not something the Bible gives us directly. They always follow something else which has gone before.

The classic statement of this was made by our Lord in His Sermon on the Mount, where He said, "Blessed are they which do hunger and thirst after"—happiness, joy, peace? Not at all—"blessed are they which do hunger and thirst after *righteousness:* for they shall be filled" (Mt 5:6, emphasis added). In other words, if you make happiness or joy or peace your one aim and object in life, it is certain you will never find them; but if you put righteousness as your main aim and if you become so concerned about righteousness and true living that you can be said to be hungering and thirsting after it, well then, says our Lord, you will be filled with happiness; it is something that follows.

This, I think you will agree with me, is something

that is absolutely vital and fundamental. If you come to the Christian faith merely because of what you want it to do, you will never get that thing, nor will you get anything else. The Bible must be taken in its own way, it must be accepted on its own terms; there are no shortcuts once you begin to deal with God. God demands something which is central from us; He demands a total allegiance. You cannot take things out of the Gospel of Christ. You must take the Gospel as it is without any modification or qualification. So if you want blessedness you must start with righteousness, otherwise you will never know it.

*I*f *you want blessedness you must start with righteousness.* ∾

Now we have here another example and illustration of that selfsame thing. "Let not your heart be troubled"—do you want a quiet heart? "Very well," says our Lord in effect to these men, "I am not going to discuss with you a *direct* means of obtaining the quiet heart. If you want that this is what you must do: 'Believe in God, believe also in me.'" Before we begin to consider our initial states and conditions; before we begin to consider our life in this world, the Bible invites us to consider our relationship to God. I think it is obvious why the world is as it is today; it is because men and women are all trying to obtain happiness directly. We are leaving out the fundamental principles, and we are doomed to failure and disappointment. We must start at the very beginning. This is the very beginning. So we shall not discuss any more the means and methods to happiness and peace and joy; the cults will do that. No, the Bible says we should desire to have righteousness. It takes us right out of our little narrowly confined, rather selfish interest, and it says, "Before you discuss together whether you are happy or not, we will start by discussing *you*, and you in your relationship to God."

Let us, then, look at it like this: What does belief in God mean? It is one of those fundamental things that we tend to take for granted. We say, "I always have believed in God." But the disciples believed in God in that way and our Lord knew that perfectly well. But if those disciples had really been believing in God, they would not have been unhappy. To have a troubled heart means that you are not believing in God truly. There is something wrong in your belief; otherwise you would not be like that. There is nothing more fatal than to assume these things. "Of course I believe in God!" we say, but are we certain that we do?

If those disciples had really been believing in God, they would not have been unhappy. To have a troubled heart means that you are not believing in God truly. ❧

An alternative way of asking that question is to put it the other way round. Is your heart at rest, as you look at yourself and contemplate the state of the world? Is there peace in your soul as you look into the future and try to visualise yourself if certain things were to come to pass? We have considered these, the ills of life, and all the various things that come and disturb our equanimity. So the vital question to ask is, have we peace of heart, is it ready to face all and to go through? That is what matters.

When we read Hebrews 11 and take a walk through that gallery of the heroes of the faith, we see men and women who lived in this world, exactly as we do. Yet the whole thing about them is that they lived their lives in an entirely different manner from other people. They triumphed, they went through, they had a joy and a peace and a happiness that all the things they had to endure could not disturb. Therefore, the way to approach this question is to discover their secret; what was it that enabled them to do this? Well, the author of Hebrews really gives a key to the answer in the sixth verse of chapter 11, where he puts it like this: "He that cometh to God must believe that he is, and that he is a rewarder of them that diligently seek him." And that is just another way of saying what our Lord says here: "Let not your heart be troubled:... believe in God."

So, then, what does that mean? Well, there in Hebrews we are reminded that the first thing at any rate is to "believe that he is"; we must believe in the existence of God. If you are uncertain of the being and existence of God, you will never have a quiet heart; it is impossible. I do not hesitate to make that dogmatic statement, for I think I was able to show you earlier that it is true in this way, that the people who do not believe in God try to produce a kind of peace by not thinking at all. But that is not the solution, that is drugging yourself, that is hitting yourself on the head and knocking your brain out of action. And while you are unconscious you are not actively suffering, and enduring pain. Refusing to think just evades the problem. The Bible challenges it, and says that without thus believing in God, the quiet heart is impossible. "There is no peace, saith my God, to the wicked" (Is 57:21), and the wicked, ultimately, are those who do not truly believe in Him.

> F*irst we must believe that God is from eternity to eternity; God is not a created being, God IS.* ✍

So we believe that He is, and that means first we must believe that God is from eternity to eternity; God is not a created being, God *is.* Of course we enter into a realm here where our minds begin to boggle; we cannot understand. We are entirely limited to the book which we call the Bible; there we have the revelation of this great being who tells us that there is no beginning to Him. There is no start to God; He is life, He is everything, God the absolute and the eternal one, from everlasting to everlasting. You cannot prove the being of God, you just take the revelation and you accept it; if you could prove it, it would mean that your mind is of necessity bigger than God Himself, so to believe in Him is to believe in His eternity.

It is likewise to believe in His might and power, and

in His glory. God is almighty, He is all-powerful. His glory is such that no human being can approach unto Him. He dwells in light, the glory of God is beyond thought and imagination. We must believe that about Him and we must believe in the so-called "attributes" of God—that He knows everything, that He is present everywhere, that nothing happens without His knowledge and apart from His sight. He is omniscient, omnipresent, almighty; and added to that we must believe that He is absolutely holy. There are great terms which are given in the Bible to describe this holiness—"God is light, and in him is no darkness at all" (1 Jn 1:5); He is "the Father of lights, with whom is no variableness, neither shadow of turning" (Jas 1:17); "For our God is a consuming fire" (Heb 12:29)—those are the terms that are given and they are all just an expression of utter, absolute holiness, entirely apart from sin. He not only tempts no one with evil, but neither can He be tempted; He is in eternal brightness and perfection and beauty. We must believe that about God.

Then we must believe that He is the maker of everything that is; He has brought everything into being. The cosmos has not just happened; it has not come out of nothing and from nowhere, it is God who has set it upon its course. He is the originator and the artificer, the author and the creator and indeed the sustainer of everything that is, whether animate or inanimate.

This is part, at any rate, of what the Bible means by believing in God. It means, therefore, that God controls everything. You see, if the secret of the quiet heart ultimately is to believe in God, then I must believe in addition that nothing happens apart from Him. Yes, and beyond that, I must believe that He is able to do everything; that there is nothing too hard for the Lord.

> *I*f the secret of the quiet heart ulti-
> mately is to believe in God, then I
> must believe in addition that nothing
> happens apart from Him. ∾

Now you will find, as you read the Bible, that these have been very practical considerations for certain people. There was Abraham with that terrible problem over sacrificing Isaac. "What can I do about this?" he thought, "Is God able to do this?" And God said, "Yes!" And because of this, Abraham believed "that God was able to raise him [Isaac] up, even from the dead" (Heb 11:19). "With God nothing shall be impossible" (Lk 1:37), and what an essential part this is of the whole Gospel of salvation and the quiet heart that it gives. That was the answer given by the angel to Mary when he went to her with the great announcement. She said, "How can these things be? I am a virgin, I know not a man"; and that was his response: "With God nothing shall be impossible." And if you do not believe this, you will never truly know the quiet heart.

We may find ourselves in situations in which nothing and no one can help us, except this God with whom all things are possible. It is the whole basis of belief in miracles. There is a person dying; medical science has exhausted itself, has done everything it knows, with no result. But a body of simple people turn to God in prayer and faith, and ask Him to do the impossible and it happens. Miracles are an essential part of this belief. So there are preliminary things which we must believe, if we believe that God is.

But there are some other aspects of this matter. To believe in God also means to believe what He has said about life. It is all recorded in the Bible. I have already reminded you that the heroes of the faith were all facing this problem of life in the world, and that is one of the first ways in which the problem is bound to present itself to us. I face my problem and I say, "What is going to happen in this world, what is going to happen to me?" And that raises the other question in my mind: What is this world, what is this life of man, why are things as they are at this present time? I cannot have a quiet heart without facing these problems. I must have some explanation. My heart cannot be quiet, in a sense, until my mind is satisfied, and the Bible answers my mind and gives me satisfaction in telling me these things about God.

God has revealed certain things about life and He has told us that He made the world perfect. "Through faith," said the writer of Hebrews, "we understand that the worlds were framed by the word of God" (Heb 11:3); it is by faith we believe and accept it, because He tells us that. And then, of course, we go on to believe what is told us, likewise, about the fall of man and of how sin came in. Alas, an element has entered into life; it is not part of the essential life; it is something fallen. A principle of evil has entered in and that is the origin and explanation and source of all our ills and troubles. Now the Bible tells me that, and it is ultimately a part of my belief in God.

And then, of course, it goes on to tell me that in spite of all that, God, because He is also love in addition to being light and holiness and righteousness, in His infinite mercy and pity has made a proclamation, an announcement, that He is going to do something about this world. He has said that He will operate in such a way in this world and life, that out of the chaos He will again produce order.

> *I*t is still His world; He has not *turned His back upon it. He is not allowing it to sin itself into utter hope-lessness; He comes into it.* ∾

The promise was given right away at the beginning: the seed of the woman shall bruise the serpent's head (Gn 3:15). This world is not left to itself. So the essence of this biblical message, which gives us ultimately a quiet heart, is that this great God, whom I have been trying, inadequately, to describe, is intimately concerned about life in this world. It is still His world; He has not turned His back upon it. He is not allowing it to sin itself into utter hopelessness; He comes into it. So the whole message of the Bible is of God disturbing the course of life in this world and coming in as a Saviour.

"Believe in God," says our Lord. But that, of course, involves a belief in something further. God has addressed mankind and set before us two ways and He has told the world from the beginning that there are two possibilities confronting us all. There is the possibility of blessing and the alternative is cursing. God has told us that whether we have blessing or cursing depends solely upon whether our lives are lived in accordance with His way and plan, whether they are lived in obedience to Him or whether they are not. You live my way of life, says God, and you will be blessed; if you do not you will be cursed.

He said that, of course, to the children of Israel and we have their example before us. These people had been involved in the captivity of Judah; they were God's people but there they were slaves in Egypt. And God, in a miraculous manner, went down into Egypt and brought them out. As their captors were pursuing them, He destroyed them in the Red Sea. He took the children of Israel into the Promised Land where He was going to give them wonderful things, but before He did so, He addressed them and said, in effect, "I solemnly warn you that there are the two possibilities before you—blessing and cursing. If you live in the way that I tell you," said God to those people, "then 'blessing I will bless you', but if you do not, then 'cursing I will curse you'" (Dt 11:27-29).

These were God's own chosen people. But eventually, you remember, they lost their land and their temple and were thrown out among the nations—it is all prophesied in the book of Deuteronomy. And God still says that to everybody. The nation of Israel is nothing but a great example held up by God before the whole world. It is God showing us what He does to every being who is born into this life and world; it is either blessing or cursing, it is obedience or disobedience.

Now I say that God has a plan with regard to the whole of this world, a plan that He is working out slowly and yet surely. Things may seem to be taking their own course and yet that is not the case according to the Bible. God is over all; He is manipulating everything; He allows a number of things to happen, but they are not outside His control. You go back to the Old Testament and look at that nation of Israel. In the fulness of time God does what He says He is going to do. He allows things to go on until a certain fixed point. He knows the date; nobody else knows, but there is a day coming when He will bring an end to the history of this world. There will be an end of time and He will finally judge the whole world and all its people and then He will destroy all evil and we will have "new heavens and a new earth, wherein dwelleth righteousness" (2 Pt 3:13). God will have fulfilled His old promise of restoring order out of chaos, and giving universal blessing to those who belong to Him. So the vital question for us is whether we realise that it is one or the other of these two; we must believe all that, it is part of believing in God.

But I do not stop at that point, I must go on to say this: To believe in God means that we must believe implicitly in the promises of God to those who do thus

follow Him and give themselves to Him. I imagine
that this was the thing that our Lord was concerned to
impress upon the minds of those troubled disciples.
"Let not your heart be troubled:... believe in God."
Why? Well, think of the promises that God has made
to those who do believe in Him. Read the Psalms, read
the prophets, read God's gracious promises throughout the Bible. Our Lord had already reminded these
disciples of some of them. He said to them, "Fear not
them which kill the body, but are not able to kill the
soul: but rather fear him which is able to destroy both
soul and body in hell" (Mt 10:28). Do not be afraid of
men, he said, there is a limit to what they can do to
you, but fear God.

> "*Let not your heart be troubled...
> believe in God.*" Why? Well,
> *think of the promises that God has
> made to those who do believe in Him.* ∾

He also said that nothing could happen to them
apart from God. "Are not two sparrows sold for a far-
thing? and one of them shall not fall on the ground
without your Father.... Ye are of more value than many
sparrows" (Mt 10:29, 31). "The very hairs of your
head are all numbered," he told them (Mt 10:30). You
see, we are in a difficult world where things are happening to us and upsetting our hearts. Since they are
being troubled, what is the antidote? To believe in a
God who has so loved me that He has counted the

very hairs of my head; He is so concerned about me and my welfare that He knows me to that extent. When I really believe that this great Almighty God is as interested in me as that, then I know I have nothing to be afraid of and my heart need not be troubled. "All things work together for good to them that love God" (Rom 8:28)—that is another promise. *All* things, I do not care what they are. It is universal.

But, you say, how can war, or illness, or an accident, or the death of a loved one, how can these things possibly work to my good? Well, I cannot answer that in detail, but I can tell you something that will include every eventuality and possibility. If you really believe in God, anything that may happen to you will drive you nearer to God and anything that drives you nearer to Him is a "good thing" for you. I put it to your experience as I put it to my own experience; let us all be frank and honest. When life is running smoothly and easily and the sun is shining in the heavens and everything is going well, how easy it is to forget all about God. We do not seem to need Him and we forget Him and we are far away from Him. But then something goes wrong, there is an announcement of war, or there is trouble, or an accident, and these things drive me back to my knees. I then get nearer to God and "It is good for me that I have been afflicted," because "before I was afflicted I went astray" (Ps 119:71, 67), and every one of us can re-echo the sentiment of the psalmist. God sometimes has to chastise us in order to draw us back a little bit nearer to Himself.

D.L. Moody used to tell of the parents that came to him distressed because they had lost their only little child. They were unhappy and had a sense of grudge against God; their trouble was, "How can you say all things work together for good?" And Moody answered them by telling them a story of a shepherd who was trying to drive two sheep across a river and was failing; they were running in every direction and the shepherd could not get them across. Then he suddenly thought of an expedient. He took hold of the little lamb of one of these sheep and just carried the little lamb across the river and the sheep immediately followed.

> *God sometimes has to chastise us in order to draw us back a little bit nearer to Himself.* ∾

We are so foolish that God sometimes has to do things like that with us, and they are all done in love. You see He took the little child and that ultimately led to the conversion of that father and mother; and the salvation of their souls was more important even than having a dearly beloved child for a few extra years in a passing world like this—"All things work together for good to them that love God."

But He has also said, "I will never leave thee, nor forsake thee" (Heb 13:5); that is another of His promises. "Believe in God," says Christ; believe Him when He speaks to you, believe what He says. Whatever happens to you, whatever may be your experience, He has promised He will never leave you. Underneath, always, are the everlasting arms. Therefore, says the author of Hebrews, in the light of all these things, "The Lord is my helper, and I will not fear what man shall do unto me" (Heb 13:6). He has a quiet heart, you see, because he knows that the Lord is his helper. "Believe in God" means believing in the promises of God.

> He has promised He will never leave you. Underneath, always, are the everlasting arms. ❧

And the last thing it means is this: believing God thus, we are now ready to commit ourselves and our lives and our affairs into these almighty loving arms. To believe in God is to be like those men and women in Hebrews 11. This was their secret. They so believed God that they risked everything upon that belief, they banked their all upon it and they based their whole view of life upon it; they trusted Him. There was Moses who forsook the courts of Egypt and all his privileged position. Why? Because "By faith... he endured, as seeing him who is invisible"—he had his eye on "the recompense of the reward" (Heb 11:27, 26)—he believed God. And Abraham had done the same thing long before. He came out of his ancestral home not knowing where he was going. Why did he do it? Because he believed God and had implicit faith and trust in Him. And that has been the story and the experience of all the saints right down the running centuries. To believe God means an utter, implicit confidence in what He has said about Himself and in what He has said about what He will do. It means casting yourself entirely upon that: "Let not your heart be troubled:... believe in God."

> To believe God means an utter, implicit confidence in what He has said about Himself and in what He has said about what He will do. ◌

Yes, but there is still more! Jesus Christ also comes in—"Believe in God, believe also in me," he says. There are difficulties about believing in God and God knows that, so He sent His only begotten Son into this world to live as a man amongst men and women and He, looking at these disciples said, in effect, "You find that to believe in God thus is hard and difficult? Well, look at me again, believe in me also, trust me. If you trust me, you are trusting God; seeing me you are seeing the Father. 'I am the way, the truth, and the life: no man cometh unto the Father, but by me'" (Jn 14:6). There it is in its essence. He is the guarantee of everything that God has said.

Believe in God, believe in His Son, the Lord Jesus Christ, and commit yourself and your ways entirely to Him.

THREE

"Believe Also in Me"

❧

Then saith he to Thomas,
"reach hither thy finger, and behold my hands....
Be not faithless, but believing."
And Thomas answered and said unto him,
My Lord and my God!
John 20:27-28

WE FIRST OF ALL GLANCED at the false ways of seeking the quiet heart, because, as I have already suggested, this is not only the great need of mankind, it is the quest of the whole of mankind. Everybody in the world, somehow or other, is looking for this peace. Some do it in a very rowdy manner, but still what they are looking for is the quiet heart. They indulge in shouting and in clamouring and that is, of course, simply to try to silence and to drown the voice of disturbance, and perhaps of anguish, that is speaking within them.

Thus it comes to pass very often that appearances are most deceptive; people who look as if they were supremely happy and carefree have what is sometimes called a "skeleton in the cupboard." They are full of some great grief and carry a tragedy in their own bosoms. We put on a bold face very often and sometimes it is exceptionally bold because of the acuteness of the problem which is within. So it follows that anyone who is truly Christian will never take people merely as they appear to be, but will feel a great sense of sorrow for men and women who are trying vainly to find the quiet heart by refusing to think. This includes all the people who plunge into a round of pleasure, who give themselves to the cults and commit intellectual suicide, who rush away for treatment to some psychologist or other, who drug themselves or take up certain ancient Eastern religions. All are simply trying somehow or other to find this peace which ever seems to elude them, this quiet heart that never seems to become an actuality.

But, of course, we do not stop at it negatively like that; we are concerned to give a positive exposition of what the Bible has to tell us about this vital and all-important subject, and I would remind you again that the Bible claims that it and it alone can really show us this quiet heart. I do not apologise for that, I state and assert it.

> We *cannot mix the Gospel of Jesus Christ with anything else, it is either this or nothing. No compromise.* ⌒

We cannot mix the Gospel of Jesus Christ with anything else, it is either this or nothing. No compromise, no coalition is possible. Unless we realise that we have to submit and surrender ourselves entirely to God's way, we shall never, as we have seen, experience the blessings that he has to give us. Our Lord constantly said that very thing. He lays it down at the very beginning that this is the way to know His love and His blessing: "If any man will come after me, let him deny himself, and take up his cross, and follow me" (Mt 16:24)—that is it. The two words "follow me" in a sense say it all; what you have to do is to forsake yourself and everything else and go after Him; His claim is for a total allegiance.

Let us, then, continue to consider together the Bible's method of giving us a quiet heart. This, the Bible tells us, is an actual and practical possibility for us in this world of time. I have reminded you of those wonderful people, of whom we are given a glimpse in Hebrews 11, men and women like ourselves who went through life with a peace and rest and quietness of heart that nothing could disturb. Furthermore, we are fortified in our consideration of all this by the long history and record of the Christian Church. This is not theory, it is something that has been verified so often in the lives of men and women. I never tire of saying that there is nothing more exhilarating than to read the lives of God's people throughout the ages. Countless numbers of them all join in testifying to this truth, which is the truth of God, and which works in experience.

You can pick up the biographies of any of the men and women of God who have lived in this life, as you and I are living, who have known terrible troubles and trials but who have been able to testify that in the midst of it all, their hearts were perfectly quiet. The great stories of the saints and the martyrs and the confessors and, too, the great stories of many ordinary people in the Church of God all testify to the same thing.

Now that is what I have to offer. It is my privilege to tell you that it is possible for you, whatever your position, whatever your circumstance and condition and problem, to be delivered from trouble and distress and from pain of mind and of heart, and to know the peace of God "which passeth all understanding." I want to put this before you as an actuality and as a possibility, here and now.

> *It is possible for you... whatever your circumstance... to be delivered from trouble and distress and from pain of mind and of heart, and to know the peace of God "which passeth all understanding."* ∾

So how is this to be obtained? Well, we have seen that the great principle which we must lay down is that this is something that is to be obtained indirectly and not directly, and the biblical method of doing this is not to consider our troubles but to start immediately with God. "Let not your heart be troubled"—why? "Believe in God." Immediately you are taken out of yourself, and you are confronting Him. Half our troubles in this matter lie in the fact that the world is too much with us; we are in the midst of it, we are immersed by it all and we are lost in the details. So what the Bible really does with us, in the first instance, is just to take hold of us and drag our attention away from the immediate scene to God. This is not escapism, because having got us to confront God and His Son, it brings us back to the problem and then it enables us to overcome it.

And that is why the biblical method is such a healthy one. How different it is from many of the psychotherapeutic methods which, sometimes for years, delve into you and your experiences, and make you talk about yourself and bring up your past and so on. The Bible does not need to know all the details of our past life; it knows already that our fundamental need is God, so it begins to talk about Him. That is where we must start. We have already considered together what was meant by that.

But now we must go forward a step; "Believe in God," yes, but "believe also in me," says Jesus Christ. Here again is something that is absolutely vital so let me try to put it to you as a number of propositions. The first is that belief in the Lord Jesus Christ is the specific Christian message. Now I put it like that, briefly, because if we are not clear about that at the very outset, we must go wrong everywhere else. It is almost incredible, but it is still true to say that there are large numbers of people who seem to think that being a Christian is to believe in God in general. They say that they are Christians but when you ask them on what grounds, their answer is simply that they believe in God. Or they may say that they believe in a spiritual realm or in prayer, but they do not mention the Lord Jesus Christ, they have nothing to say about Him. But that is not to be a Christian at all! Surely, by definition, to be a Christian means to believe something about this person, Jesus of Nazareth, the Lord Jesus Christ.

> T*here are large numbers of people who seem to think that being a Christian is to believe in God.* ❧

The Gospel of Jesus Christ, in other words, in its specific message, is something that brings us face to face with Him; there is no sense or meaning in the term "Christian" apart from that. The Jew believes in God, so does the Mohammedan, but they are not Christian because Jesus Christ has not entered in. The differentiating thing about the Gospel is that it brings us immediately and directly into relationship with Him, and what it emphasises at this point is that we must believe in Him as we believe in God the Father. This is the particular point that makes Christianity, Christianity.

Now you notice that the Gospel does not ask us to believe certain things about His teaching; it does not ask us to follow Him in the matter of teaching. No, He says, in essence, "As you believe in God, believe also in me. Put the same faith and trust in me as you do with God the Father; believe also in me as I exhort you to believe in Him." In other words, this person Jesus is absolutely vital and essential to the Christian method of obtaining the quiet heart; and what I have to do, therefore, is to ask you to look with me once more at Him.

> This person Jesus is absolutely vital
> and essential to the Christian
> method of obtaining the quiet heart. ✧

Now our text is, after all, history, it is something that has happened. There was once a person on the face of this earth called Jesus of Nazareth, and here, looking at a body of men, He says in effect, "If you are going to have a quiet heart, if you are to enjoy peace and rest, if you are going to go through all that is coming to you with a quiet heart, undisturbed and even rejoicing, you must believe in me, as you believe in God the Father." And that is still the essence of the Christian message.

Do you have a quiet heart? Is it at rest at this moment, or are you troubled and disturbed; are you worried, perhaps, about your past, something you did yesterday, during the week, or last year? Is there something troubling your conscience, making you restless and ill at ease? How do you feel with respect to the future? Is there something you know is going to happen in your life or experience or in your family that is going to make you unhappy? Are you face to face with some great change in your circumstances: are you perhaps looking at the illness or the death of a dear one; is there business trouble or worry; is your own health troubling you; is the future just something that is full of concern to you?

Perhaps you are disturbed about what you read in your newspaper, and what you hear elsewhere, as to the possible things that may be awaiting us—is there going to be another war and, if there is, how is it going to affect me? Is that your problem or trouble? I ask you, Are you at rest and peace, do you know what to do when these things come to meet you suddenly? Do you know how to find tranquillity and poise and balance, and even joy, in addition to rest and quiet? Have you the secret, have you found it?

Those are the questions. We have to face that this is the real problem of life and living. It is the one starting point in discussion about the Christian faith. As far as I am concerned, I am not going to discuss the Lord Jesus Christ with people until I have talked to them about themselves, and what I want to know about them is this: *Where do you stand at this moment*? Because I must tell you that if you do not have a quiet heart, the real reason is that you do not know this person who says, "Believe also in me."

So then, let us look at Him together. What does believing in Him mean; what does he mean when He says this? Let me summarise it.

To believe in (or on) the Lord Jesus Christ, is something that I can only discover as I read my New Testament. Someone may say, "What am I to believe about this person? I do want that quiet heart, but you say I must believe in Him before I can obtain it; so what are you asking me to do?" Now I say that we must, of necessity, come to the New Testament for the answer to that question. I know nothing about the Lord Jesus Christ, except what I find there. There are so many people who say, "I believe this and that about Him and this is what I think." But they say that independent of the best source of information.

Let me emphasise that I not only go to the four Gospels in order to discover the truth about Him; I also go to the book of the Acts of the Apostles. I also go to the Epistles; indeed, there is a sense in which I am prepared to say that I should go to Acts and the Epistles before I go to the Gospels. I suggest to you that there are many people who are confused about the person of the Lord Jesus Christ because they stop in the Gospels and never go out of them. You will never know Him truly as long as you do that.

He said Himself, as we find it recorded in the Gospels, that there were certain things He could not say to His followers and disciples while He was still with them. "I have yet many things to say unto you," He said, "but ye cannot bear them now" (Jn 16:12). You see, they could not understand His death until He had passed through it all. He said, "It is all right, I will send the Holy Ghost, the Comforter, and He will explain all these things to you."

And let us never forget that the things that are recorded in the book of Acts had happened before these Gospels were ever written. Let us remember also that the first preachers of the Christian message did not preach out of the four Gospels; there were no such things. They went round preaching about Jesus Christ of Nazareth who, they said, was the Christ of God; and it was only later that the Gospels were written to those who believed and were incorporated into the churches.

> There are many people who are con-
> fused about the person of the Lord
> Jesus Christ because they stop in the
> Gospels and never go out of them. ℃

So if we want to know exactly what believing in Him means, we must take the entire New Testament, the Acts and the Epistles and the light they cast upon Him, as well as the detailed records we have concerning Him in the four Gospels. And, of course, another advantage in doing it that way is that we find so many of the Gospel details confirmed in the stories of the disciples themselves; it was only afterwards, in a sense, that they came really to understand. You remember how Peter at Caesarea Philippi made his great statement, "Thou art the Christ, the Son of the living God" (Mt 16:16), and yet you know how he denied Him afterwards. But after he had passed through Pentecost and seen the risen Lord, what a difference there was, what a different outlook! And that is the same position from which you and I can look at the Lord Jesus Christ now, and thank God for it!

What, then, do we find? Here is one in this world of time who claims that He can give men and women a quiet heart, so the first question we ask is: Who is He?

If I am not right about the person who uttered these words, I cannot be right about anything concerning Him, and I can never know what He has to give me. So we must start with Him. And the answer to that question, which is given by the entire New Testament, is that he is none other than the eternal Son of God. Now obviously this is something staggering in its immensity, something that is really baffling to the ordinary human mind, but it is the assertion of the Scriptures and we must, of necessity, start at this point.

Now the Gospels have their evidence with regard to that matter. They give us the account of His birth; they tell us that it was not an ordinary, natural birth; that He was born of a virgin, that He did not have a human Father but that He was conceived by the Holy Spirit. Do not be foolish enough to try to understand that, you never will; that is the miracle, that is an act of God. But the assertion is that He was conceived of the Holy Spirit and born of the Virgin Mary. He was not a man like other men, He came into this world from eternity, in an entirely different manner. But nevertheless we are told that He really was born as a baby, that he was truly man though He is the eternal Son of God. We are also told that He grew "in wisdom and stature, and in favour with God and man" (Lk 2:52), that He lived life as a man here on earth, limiting Himself deliberately in order to do so. The accounts of His birth are amazing. "But," you say, "the Gospel according to St. John does not give an account of His birth." John puts it like this: "In the beginning was the Word, and the Word was with God, and the Word was God" (Jn 1:1), and that eternal Word "was made flesh, and dwelt among us" (Jn 1:14). That is John's way of saying the same thing—the miracle of the Incarnation.

> **H**e really was born as a baby. He was truly man though He is the eternal Son of God. ⌁

And then the New Testament goes on to provide us with evidence concerning His teaching and His claims; you get that in this very chapter which we are considering together. He did not hesitate to say, "I am the way, the truth, and the life; no man cometh unto the Father, but by me" (Jn 14:6). Thank God for those disciples and for their stumbling, blundering minds, their scepticism and their unbelief. I thank God for a man like Philip who said to our Lord, "Look here, you are talking about the Father, show us the Father and it is enough for us"; and He looked at him and said, "Have I been so long time with you, and yet hast thou not known me, Philip? He that hath seen me hath seen the Father" (v. 9). We need to have it explained, to remedy our unbelief.

He does not hesitate to say, "Ye have heard it was said by them of old time,... But *I* say unto you" (Mt 5:27-28, emphasis added); "I and my Father are one" (Jn 10:30); "He that receiveth me receiveth him that sent me" (Mt 10:40); "Before Abraham was, I am" (Jn 8:58)—oh! go through these Gospels for yourselves, look at His words and teaching! Look at His claims. I have already reminded you that His claim calls for a total allegiance on the part of men and women. Here was one who did not hesitate to say to others, "Follow me," leave everything, leave your father and your business, as it were, and come after me. He comes to a man sitting at the receipt of custom and He says to him, "Follow me," (Mt 9:9)—and he does!

And then there are the miracles that are recorded here. He makes use of that very argument in talking to doubting Thomas and doubting Philip; "Believe me," he says, "that I am in the Father, and the Father in me: or else believe me for the very works' sake" (Jn 14:11). "Look at what I am doing," he says in effect; "look at the evidence of the miracles!"

D*o you want a quiet heart? Well, it involves a belief in the miracles and in Him who worked these miracles.* ❧

These miracles are recorded in the four Gospels because they tell us something about this person. They are facts, they have happened and they are all part of the testimony and witness to Him. Do you want a quiet heart? Well, it involves a belief in the miracles and in Him who worked these miracles, and I challenge anyone who does not believe that, because you will never have a quiet heart without believing in Him; and to believe in Him includes believing in His miracles, these things which are attested and which proclaim Him to be the Son of God.

But, of course, we do not stop at that, and this is where it is so vital to go on and look at His death and resurrection. Here is the astounding thing about it; here was one who made exalted claims, but who was crucified in utter helplessness and His dead body was put into a grave. "There is the end," said everybody, but on the morning of the third day, they found the grave empty, and He began to appear to His disciples and His chosen followers. They met together one night in a closed room for fear of the Jews, when suddenly, without the door opening, "He stood in the midst" and said, "Look at me," and He sat down and ate broiled fish and a honeycomb with them (Lk 24:36, 43). "Declared," says the apostle Paul, "to be the Son of God with power, according to the spirit of holiness, by the resurrection from the dead" (Rom 1:4). It was that which finally convinced these men; it was that which finally proved that he was the Son of God, and that is why they went round, in the book of Acts, preaching "Jesus and the resurrection," the Resurrection that proclaimed Him to be the Son of God and therefore the Messiah and the Saviour of the world.

Then there is His Ascension, and, finally, as we read in Acts 2, His sending of the Holy Spirit upon the infant Church there at Jerusalem on the day of Pentecost is a kind of postscript to it all. Furthermore, there is His appearance to Saul of Tarsus on the road to Damascus, as "one born out of due time" (1 Cor 15:8), to give the evidence that made him an apostle and made him proclaim the Son of God as Saviour of the world—Jesus the Son of God.

Now that is the evidence which we have provided for us in the New Testament, and all the great arguments which you find in the various epistles show exactly the same thing. That is what it means to believe in Jesus—we believe all that about Him. Or let me put it like this: I am asked to believe that into the very midst of the turmoil and the chaos and the unhappiness and the misery of this sinful world, the Son of God has come. Do you not see that this is the very essence of the Gospel?

> D*o you want a quiet heart? Here is the way to have one, to believe that God has come to us in the person of His Son. We... are not left to grope vainly in the dark.* ✿

Do you want a quiet heart? Here is the way to have one, to believe that God has come to us in the person of His Son. We are not left on the human level; we are not left to grope vainly in the dark. God has done something and this is what He has done: He has "sent forth his Son, made of a woman, made under the law, to redeem them that were under the law" (Gal 4:4-5), and that He might give us this quiet heart.

That is the first thing, to believe the truth concerning Him and His person. What is the second step? It is to consider *why* He came. We cannot deal with that in detail now, because it is the theme, in a sense, of this entire chapter 14 of John's Gospel, but I can perhaps summarise it for you. He came to do certain things for us without which we cannot possibly have this quiet heart. He came to reveal God to us as the Father. Yes, the Old Testament saints did know something about God as Father, but not with the fulness that is possible to men and women who believe on the Lord Jesus Christ. They saw it "afar off" (Heb 11:13), but we can see it immediately and directly. He has revealed the Father— "No man hath seen God at any time; the only begotten Son, which is in the bosom of the Father, he hath declared him" (Jn 1:18). That is John's message.

I will tell you what is still more wonderful and still more passing strange. He not only tells us things about God, He brings us to God, into a living relationship. He is the one who makes us children of God and therefore puts us into this particular relationship to God; and it is through Him, and through Him alone, that we obtain the gift of the Holy Spirit, which is vital to this question of obtaining the tranquil and quiet heart. It is He who really enables us to pray because He is our great high priest and representative; He goes on to deal with that in this chapter. And finally, you remember, He offers us in this chapter, His peace: "Peace," He says, "I leave with you, my peace I give unto you: not as the world giveth, give I unto you. Let not your heart be troubled, neither let it be afraid" (Jn 14:27).

That is but a summary of the wonderful things which He has come into this world to do and to give to mankind. The key to it all, you see, is to start with the person of Jesus Christ and to be perfectly clear about Him. I can never be at peace truly until I am in the right relationship to God, and the only one who can put me in that right relationship is the Lord Jesus Christ. I will never get my sins dealt with apart from Him. I can never be a child of God and a member of the family of God and expect God to work upon me and give me His own nature and His own life, and I cannot pray—I can do none of these things. But He gives me all of them and thus He enables me to obtain this quiet heart.

I can never be at peace truly until I am in the right relationship to God, and the only one who can put me in that right relationship is the Lord Jesus Christ. ❧

Now I hope to show you later something of the work of the Lord Jesus Christ for us in our redemption and salvation. But we have been looking at the person Himself, so let us close by looking still at Him. This is what is offered to us in Him. Here are we, on earth, in this difficult modern world with all its problems, its trials, and its perplexities. We are conscious of weakness and of failure; we are conscious of the fact that the whole thing is too vast, too immense for us. What can we do? "Believe in God," I say. "Well yes," you say, "I want to believe in God, but He is so distant, He is great and almighty, He is so holy and eternal, what can I do to bridge the gap, to reach Him?"

And the answer of the author of the Epistle to the Hebrews is that, there in the presence of God, we have a most sympathetic high priest and representative, none other than this blessed person who looked into the face of His disciples and said, "Let not your heart be troubled:... believe in God, believe also in me." Let us realise that, seated at the right hand of God in glory at this very moment, is one who has been in this world. He knows the sorrows of the human heart, He knows your weakness and your frailty. What a difference that makes to us! He knows all about you, so you can venture to come to Him.

We are in this life, says the author of Hebrews, but He gives "grace to help in time of need" (Heb 4:16). When all things seem against us to drive us to despair, we do not know what to do, and we cry out, "How can we have this grace?" Here is the blessed answer: There is one seated at the right hand of God who understands it all perfectly, He "was in all points tempted like as we are, yet without sin" (Heb 4:15). He has been among us, He knows it exactly. Read the Gospels again; look at Him. He never missed a case of suffering. He never passed by in a hurry when men and women were in anguish. The disciples tried to stop those women bringing their infants in arms for Him to bless them, but He said, It is all right, do not stop them, "Suffer the little children to come unto me, and forbid them not" (Mk 10:14). The poor blind man outside Jericho was crying out, "Jesus, thou Son of David, have mercy on me," and everyone tried to silence him, but our Lord was not in a hurry. He was going up to Jerusalem and what I read about Him is that He stood still. He called them to bring the man to Him and He healed him (Mk 10:46-52). He always had time to take trouble.

Then when He was dying and enduring that terrible agony upon the Cross, even then He had time to speak to the thief dying at His side, and to tell him not to be troubled because he should be with Him that day in paradise (Lk 23:39-43). There was never such a tender, gentle heart; there was never one who had such compassion and an eye for the suffering of those who were out of the way; there was never one who came down so low, a friend of publicans and sinners.

He is still the same, He has not changed. John in his vision on the Isle of Patmos saw Him in His glory, and yet He was still the same. He is still the same in your need, in your trouble, in your agony. When your heart is restless and when you are troubled and when you are disturbed, go to Him. He said when He was here, "Him that cometh to me I will in no wise cast out" (Jn 6:37), and He is still the same. He will understand you, He will sympathise with you, He will give you all you need, and you will lose your trouble; and He will give you His own peace "which passeth all understanding" (Phil 4:7). "Believe in God, believe also in me."

PART II
The Soul and Its Future

"In my Father's house are many mansions:
if it were not so, I would have told you.
I go to prepare a place for you.
And If I go and prepare a place for you,
I will come again, and receive you unto myself;
that where I am, there ye may be also. "
JOHN 14:2-3

FOUR

"In My Father's House"

&

And I will dwell in the house of the Lord for ever.
Psalm 23:6

IN OUR CONSIDERATION OF HOW we may obtain the quiet heart, we have seen that the first thing our Lord emphasises is our relationship to God. When you face life, says the Bible everywhere, if you want to face it truly, you must, for the time being, turn your back on the problem and turn to God.

In other words, according to the Bible, you can only face life truly in the light of something else. The trouble with us is that with our limited perspective we let life overwhelm us, but the way to understand it is to step out of it and look down upon it. It seems to me comparable to those aerial photographs. A very good way of getting to understand and know a section of country is to look at an aerial photograph, or if you cannot do that, to climb a mountain and then look down upon the vast expanse. That is the way to grasp the whole thing; it is much better than walking along the roads in the valley. You get the right angle and perspective. It is the whole view of life that is really tremendously important as I hope to show you. Most people are defeated by life because they take a piecemeal view of it, instead of looking at it as a whole.

So, our Lord and Saviour teaches us this at this point by saying first of all that you start with God: "Believe in God." Not only must you believe certain things about God, you must believe in Him, you must take Him at His word, you must trust Him, you must have confidence in Him. Hudson Taylor, the great founder of the China Inland Mission,[1] always insisted that the right translation of what we read in the Authorised Version (KJV) as "have faith in God," really is: "hold on to the faithfulness of God." That is really believing in God; it is not a belief in your faith or belief itself, that is important. No, hold on to the faithfulness of God; have faith in Him, be certain of Him, for you will never master and conquer life in this world until, in spite of everything, you do hold on in that way.

> "**H**old on to the faithfulness of God." That is really believing in God; it is not a belief in your faith or belief itself. ∾

That is the great argument of Romans 8, where Paul, with his mighty logic, puts it like this: You can be certain of God for this reason; "He that spared not his own Son, but delivered him up for us all"—who gave

---

1. Now the Overseas Missionary Fellowship

Him to the death of the Cross—"how shall he not with him also freely give us all things?" (Rom 8:32). That is the certainty of God and you must start with that.

Then, secondly, you must be absolutely certain about the Lord Jesus Christ and believe the vital truths concerning Him. His whole argument here; as we shall see, depends upon those things; that is the very comfort He is administering. "If you do not believe me," says our Lord in effect, "and believe that I am going to do certain things for you, then I have no comfort to give you. But if you do believe, then you will have a quiet heart, and your hearts need not be troubled."

The next logical step is none other than obtaining a right view of our life in this world. That is the order, steps one, two, and three. We tend to start with the third step, we tackle the problem of life in the world. But consider the Christian way of approaching it: You do not rush at your problem; no, you go right away back. Picture yourself confronted by a great hurdle. You want to get over it to reach something else beyond it. Now, ultimately, the right way to get over that hurdle is to go back first. "But," says someone, "doesn't that seem foolish?" Yes, but that is the way— you go back, then you turn and run. Having got this momentum you clear the hurdle! And that is the biblical method everywhere. Do not go immediately to your problem, start further back.

Put it like this: if you are confronted by a problem of the unknown, a very good rule is to start with the known; that is a favourite method in scientific research.

Go from the known to the unknown. Do not start with the unknown immediately, start further back where you are sure of certain postulates. Lay them down. Then, having built up your case, go on to the inevitable result which must follow from it. That is exactly the method which our Lord is, in a sense, employing here. First God, then the Lord Jesus Christ, *then* you begin to approach your problem more directly as you come to your view of life in this world.

As we come to look at this, I am anxious to put it to you in three main propositions. The first is that life in this world can only be viewed truly in the light of the next world. Jesus says, "Let not your heart be troubled: ye believe in God, believe also in me. In my Father's house are many mansions." You see how immediately, when considering the problem of life in this world, He goes to the next. That is very characteristic of the biblical method. It is once more this question of perspective and angle and view, and therefore, we have to follow it.

> L*ife in this world can only be*
> *viewed truly in the light of the*
> *next world.* ❧

Here we are in this difficult, troubled world of ours, wondering what is going to happen, hearing of rumours and alarms, wondering what is before us and how we will get through. How are we going to live? How are we to face that? Well, Jesus says that, for a moment at any rate, we should look at the next world and then come back to this one. Now I know very well that when I say a thing like that I am saying something that is distasteful to the majority of modern people. "Ah that is it," they say, "once more it is the old story of 'pie in the sky'; you Christian people are not realistic."

That is what has frequently been said during the last hundred years or so. This is the attitude of men and women towards Christianity; they say that they are practical people and what they want is something to help them to live in this world. They are not interested in "pie in the sky"; they want some kind of practical life programme from the Gospel and the Christian Church. We have heard a great deal of that.

> *Whether we like it or not, life itself has a way of forcing us all to consider what lies beyond it.* ✻

Of course, whether we like it or not, life itself has a way of forcing us all to consider what lies beyond it. Perhaps in earlier times life was so leisurely and so complacent and quiet that men and women really regarded it as something almost permanent and ever-lasting. So all their energies and attention were directed to living life in this world and if you talked about death and the life beyond, that was really unnec-essary. But we, in our folly, have turned our backs upon God and the spiritual and we are trying to settle down in this earthly life. Suddenly came these world wars that destroyed everything, forcing us to think of the beyond.

I cannot but think that it is a judgement that we have brought upon ourselves. We are beginning to see some point in considering the whole transitory nature of life in this world.

Now the Bible has always invited us to do that; it has always asked us to start in that way. So let me expound to you now what the Bible has to say about life in this world: It is temporary and transitory. It is nothing but a great journey, something through which we are passing. We, according to the Bible, are but pilgrims and strangers in this world; we are but sojourners. This is put in a classic phrase in the Epistle to the Hebrews: "Here have we no continuing city" (Heb 13:14). It is the great message of the Bible from beginning to end. We are moving through, we are pilgrims and strangers, travellers, journeymen.

But it also goes on to remind us of something else; life is also full of uncertainty and of accidents. The Bible always does that; it does bring us face to face with the facts. The realism of the Bible in which I glory says that life is a kind of existence in which you never know what is going to happen next; just when we are safest things begin to happen. And the tragedy of the twentieth century is that we have turned our backs upon the biblical view. You see, we really did believe that by political enactments, international relationships and things like that, we could make life in this world absolutely secure and certain. So we have our pension schemes and our schemes for national health—I am not detracting from the value of such things; all I am saying is that we have been trying to persuade ourselves that we can make a certainty of life. But we cannot! You read this book of life, the Bible, and that is one of its prominent messages.

Then, of course, its next step is to show that no security can be obtained, or is promised, in this life as such, and that to live for this life only and to rely upon it, or anything in it, is deliberately to court disappointment. You find this depressing? Well, if you do, all I have to say to you is that I am just accurately describing life, and to disregard facts is, surely, to be unintelligent.

> *If we are depending for happiness and joy and a quiet heart, in a final sense, upon any individual human being, upon our family, our home, our profession, our money, our health and strength, we are doomed to disappointment.* ❧

The Bible tells us that in this life and world there is no such thing as final security apart from the message of the Gospel. So if we are relying for our final, ultimate happiness upon anybody or anything in this world alone, then we are certain to be disappointed. If our quietness of heart depends—oh, let me put it with almost brutal realism—if we are depending for happiness and joy and a quiet heart, in a final sense, upon any individual human being, upon our family, our home, our profession, our money, our health and strength, we are doomed to disappointment.

Every one of these things one day must be taken from us.

Yet is it not true that we, most of us, are building our philosophies upon such things? That is why this century is such an unhappy one and the wars have shaken everything. We have been relying upon life in this world, then suddenly comes a war and shatters it all. Now the Bible pleads with us not to do that, because, as it tells us, these things are not going to last—"Here have we no continuing city" (Heb 13:14). We come, we go, things come to pass, everything is moving. "Change and decay in all around I see,"[2] everything is moving and is going to pass.

The Bible also tells us why all that is true. It is true because of sin. It was not meant to be like that, but that is exactly what sin has done. Sin makes us try to be independent of God. It sees to it that we turn our backs upon Him and forget Him, and as we are going to make life in this world last for ever, we think we can do without Him. But God comes in and says, "Thou shalt surely die" (Gn 2:17), because of our sin. Then we are afraid! If only we could abolish death, then we would make a perfect world. But the fear of death is the thing that holds the whole of mankind in its thralldom, even as we try to ignore it.

T*he most important thing for us to concentrate on is the life of the soul.* ❧

The next proposition is that because all that is true of life in this world, the most important thing for us to

---

2. Ed. note: From the hymn "Abide with Me" (or "Eventide") by Henry F. Lyte (1793-1847).

concentrate on is the life of the soul. Here I am in a world that is passing and transitory; it is a world of uncertainty. I never know what is going to happen, I never know when the end is coming, I cannot bank or rely upon anything, so what am I to do? "Well," says the Bible, "within you there is something that is bigger than life in this world. It is imperishable and it is called the soul." That is something that goes on when the body dies and the world ends; it will go on "beyond the veil." Concentrate on that! That is what matters, the soul, not the external life, but this inner life.

Now our Lord Himself, as we have seen, put that very clearly. He was sending His disciples out to preach. They were fearful and apprehensive. He told them, "Yes, it is quite possible that, because you are preaching the Gospel, men may actually kill you, but do not be afraid of them. 'Fear not them which kill the body, but are not able to kill the soul'" (Mt 10:28). If they destroy your body they cannot touch your soul. The soul is imperishable, it cannot be attacked, it is inviolable. Therefore, concentrate on the life of the soul.

Is that not the great principle taught in the Bible everywhere from beginning to end, that we must all take that long view? You remember our Lord's picture of the so-called rich fool, who had been so successful as a farmer that his very barns had become too small for him? He said, "Soul, thou hast much goods laid up for many years; take thine ease.... " All is well, look forward to a wonderful time of prosperity! "But God said unto him, Thou fool, this night thy soul shall be

86

required of thee" (Lk 12:19, 20). It is the soul that matters.

> The main function and purpose
> of life in this world is to prepare
> us for the next one. ❧

And that leads us to the last proposition with regard to life in this world as it is described in the Bible: The main function and purpose of life in this world is to prepare us for the next one. Now let us be clear about this. That does not mean escapism; it does not mean that you turn your back on this world, or that you despise life here. It does not mean that you shut yourself up in a monastery or become a monk or a hermit, not at all! You notice what I said—the *main* function. There are many other functions. Oh yes, carry on in business or in your profession or in your family life, live it to the maximum, but never forget that the main object of life in this world is to prepare us for the next. That is the whole philosophy of the Bible; it is the secret of all the saints; read again that eleventh chapter of Hebrews. The secret of every one of those men and women was that they were looking "for a city which hath foundations, whose builder and maker is God"; they were "strangers and pilgrims on the earth" (Heb 11:10, 13), and they went on in the journey preparing for that which was to come.

That, then, is the first main proposition—that life in this world is only to be understood finally in the light of the next world.

My second proposition is that life in this world can

only be truly lived and mastered, therefore, as we have a right view of that next world. We have seen that that was the secret of all who have conquered and mastered life here. We have looked at it in our Lord Himself. The author of the Epistle to the Hebrews helps us when he says, speaking of Him, "Who for the joy that was set before him endured the cross, despising the shame" (Heb 12:2). Look at the treatment that was meted out to Him while here on earth. Look at the malignity of His enemies, the bitterness of their persecution, the wrongs He suffered. Eventually there He was, being crucified, suffering agonies, and yet He goes through it all more than triumphant. Why? "For the joy that was set before him."

That has always been true of all His followers. I ask you again to think of that mighty statement in Romans 8. "Ah yes," says Paul, "I am not promising you that you won't have troubles and difficulties— 'We are accounted as sheep for the slaughter.' I am not going to tell you that you are going to have an easy time. I do not say, believe the Gospel then lie on a bed of roses for the rest of your time in this world. Not at all! Men may persecute you and try to destroy you; hell may be let loose against you, but it does not matter.... "

In all these things we are more than conquerors.... For I am persuaded, [certain] that neither death, nor life, nor angels, nor principalities, nor powers, nor things present, nor things to come, nor height, nor depth, nor any other creature, shall be able to separate us from the love of God, which is in Christ Jesus our Lord.   **Romans 8:31-39**

That is it; let the worst come! I endure it all because I am certain of what awaits me. I know I am being prepared for a life beyond this life. Indeed, it is the argument of the apostle Paul everywhere. In writing to the Philippians, he tells them that his own future is uncertain, he does not know whether he is to live or die, but he says it is immaterial to him. "For to me to live is Christ and to die is gain," for it means "to be with Christ, which is far better" (Phil 1:21, 23). Read again the lives of some of God's saints throughout the centuries and you will find that many of these people had to suffer many hardships; and yet what joy they had!

Do you remember that great hymn of Richard Baxter's? If ever a man had trouble in this life, it was he. Yet he wrote:

Lord, it belongs not to my care
Whether I die or live;
To love and serve Thee is my share,
And this Thy grace must give.

If life be long, I will be glad
That I may long obey;
If short, yet why should I be sad
To soar to endless day?

Richard Baxter, (1615-1691)

Do you sense that quiet calm? What is it based on? It is based on the certainty of where he is going. He knows what awaits him and it is true of every saint that has lived in the world.

So let us face this quite practically together. What of you? What of your view of that next world, your view of death, your view of the life that lies beyond death? Does it frighten you; does it seem strange to you; does thinking about it like this help or does it depress you? What is your view of it? That is the greatest question you can ever face. We have to face it. We cannot avoid it. What is your feeling about it? Have you this blessed certainty? Or does the thought of death and leaving this world and going on leave you with a sense of despair and fear and strangeness? That is the question. It all depends upon your view of the next world, and that of course depends ultimately upon your view of God and upon your view of the Lord Jesus Christ.

> H*ave you this blessed certainty? Or does the thought of death… leave you with a sense of despair and fear and strangeness?* ❧

What our Lord said about it to these men was this: "I am going; I am going to die and leave you and you too, eventually, will have to die; but do not be alarmed. Let not your heart be troubled. Why? Where does death lead to? It leads to my Father's house.

"You know," he said in effect, "I have never kept anything back from you; I have never withheld anything that is unpleasant. I have always spoken the truth. If it were true that you would never see me again, I would tell you, but it is not like that—I am telling you the truth about the next life."

What a spectre, what a horrible thing death is to most of us. We regard it as a terrible monster that is going to grip us. Death, we say, is the most terrible thing of all, the thing to avoid. No, says Christ, death is nothing but the door of entry to my Father's house—"In my Father's house are many mansions."

We tend to think of ourselves after death, do we not, as in some disembodied state in some great eternity where all is strange and terrible. But it is really to go home, if you are a child of God, if you are a brother or sister of the Lord Jesus Christ. God is not some terrible awful power, away in some distant eternity; He is your Father. He is one who loves you with a love you cannot imagine. Thank God for human love, but, my dear friends, our human love pales into insignificance and nothingness by the side of the love of God towards those who belong to Him. "My Father's house" is a glorious home.

But what else does it mean? It means to be with Christ. "I go," he said, "to prepare a place for you. And if I go and prepare a place for you, I will come again, and receive you unto myself; that where I am, ye may be also." Have you not sometimes felt, as you read these Gospels, that you would give the whole world and more if you could but spend an afternoon with Him. It must have been marvellous to look into His eyes and into His face, and to feel His glorious presence—what a wonderful thing! But if you believe on Him and trust Him, from the moment you die, you will spend the endless ages of eternity with Him, in the presence of this blessed person, enjoying Him, sharing His glorious life without end.

> "In my Father's house are many mansions." In other words, "There is room enough for all of you." ∾

I rather like this expression *mansions*—"In my Father's house are many mansions." In other words, "There is room enough for all of you," says Christ; "you need not be afraid; there is a place, there is room for all." A mansion—what does it suggest? Security, surrounded by a permanent dwelling place. Here in this life, I am in a tabernacle, in a tent; it is moving nightly, daily. But there I will enjoy security, stability, rest, a home fully furnished, everything prepared for me, peace and joy, everything I like to be there awaiting me; everything my heart can desire supplied in all its fulness and beyond my imagination. "In my Father's house are many mansions"; and you and I can be absolutely certain of this, "Because," he says again, "if it were not so, I would have told you—believe me, trust yourself to me."

Now I think you will agree with me that this is the thing that matters. If I know for certain that that awaits me, then I say let this world do its very worst to me; it can never touch that which abides. That is certain, that is absolute. Yes, though men may do their worst and hell may indeed be let loose, yet "there remaineth... a rest to the people of God" (Heb 4:9). "A city which hath foundations" (Heb 11:10) is above the flux of time. It is the home of God and its glory can never be tarnished or diminished.

Do you believe that? That is the only comfort, finally, in a world like this, but the way to know it for certain as regards yourself, is to believe God, to believe the Lord Jesus Christ. He has gone to prepare that place for you and He will come again and receive you unto Himself. Realise that your soul is the one thing that matters. I cannot guarantee anything about your body. Anything may happen; you may even be dead in a matter of days. But I can guarantee you about your soul. If you put your immortal soul into the safekeeping of the Son of God, it does not matter what may happen to you in this world, and, in time, when you come to the end of your life, He will be there with you, and He will take hold of you, and He will carry you through. He will open the door of the mansion he has prepared for you, and you will enter in, and begin to enjoy what you will continue to enjoy through all eternity.

> R*ealise that your soul is the one thing that matters.* ∾

So that, too, is the secret of the quiet heart; always keep that first and never forget it. However happy you may be, never forget that, because if your happiness depends upon the world, or anything in it, it is bound to come to an end. Keep that first and, having kept that first, enjoy everything else to your heart's content. Realise, above everything else, that if you are truly

Christ's, then nothing and no one will ever be able to separate you from Him, and from the love of God that is in Him. Believe in God; believe in the Lord Jesus Christ as the Son of God, as the Saviour of your soul. He has gone to prepare a place for you and you can be certain of your eternal inheritance.

FIVE

"I Go to Prepare a Place for You"

❧

And I John saw the holy city, new Jerusalem,
coming down from God out of heaven,
prepared as a bride adorned for her husband....
God Himself shall be with them....
God shall wipe away all tears from their eyes;
and there shall be no more death, neither sorrow,
nor crying, neither shall there be any more pain:
for the former things are passed away.

Revelation 21:2-4

ONE OF THE MOST OUTSTANDING characteristics of the Gospel of Jesus Christ is its extraordinary logic. This utterly confutes the idea that the Gospel is some sort of sob stuff. If you want logic, here it is: it starts by inviting you to face facts, not to ignore them and to put on a bold front and say, "All is well," when all seems not to be well. It tells you to look at life at its worst. Then it gives you these mighty propositions and it says, "Work them out." So here is the next logical step that follows on everything we have been considering. It is a crucial step.

"Yes," someone may say, "it is all very well to say there is a mansion for me in heaven, but the question that faces me is how am I going to get there?" And here is the answer: "I go to prepare a place for you. And if I go and prepare a place for you, I will come again, and receive you unto myself; that where I am, there ye may be also." Now this is, of course, one of those great crucial statements of the Gospel of our Lord Jesus Christ. Indeed let me add to that; it is one of the most wonderful things the blessed Son of God ever uttered. "I go to prepare a place for you"—the whole of the Gospel is in that statement; in that one verse is packed the whole of Christian theology and doctrine.

> "*I go to prepare a place for you*"— *the whole of the Gospel is in that statement.* ✍

Now there is nothing that is more tragic, it seems to me, in the long history of the Christian Church and her preaching of the Gospel, than the way in which this statement, of all statements, has been so frequently ignored and misunderstood. Its real truth and import is not very often even considered at all, because people take it sentimentally. Yet it is a statement that can only be understood theologically and doctrinally; we must stop and ask exactly what it means. It is a tragedy that men and women often do not do that. This is not surprising, of course, because this statement is the very central point of the Gospel. It is one which Satan, the adversary of man's soul, has been particularly anxious to confuse and to confound. There has, therefore, been much trouble and dispute and debate over it.

Here, then, is our Lord turning to these disciples and saying, "I am going to die," and immediately they are troubled. Why? It is because they do not understand what His going and dying means. I wonder whether we are any clearer about it. What is the meaning of the death of Jesus Christ? That is the question. What does it mean to you?

There are many who would say that it is the greatest tragedy the world has ever known, but they stop at that. They say it is nothing but the tragedy of a teacher who was misunderstood because He was ahead of His time. There are some who regard it as just the death of a martyr; because of the enmity and jealousy of the Pharisees and scribes and the Jewish doctors of the Law, they say, he was condemned to death. The world was not good enough for Him. It was nothing but a great human tragedy, like Socrates. The world has always had its great martyrs and Jesus of Nazareth happened to be one of them. Others say it was nothing but the death of a political agitator. Jesus, they say, had come to deliver His fellow countrymen from the Roman yoke but the Roman authorities instigated a plot and did away with Him.

Now all these explanations would have us believe that this is nothing but the death of a *man*, a martyr, a great teacher. There are various other ideas that have been put forward which more or less correspond to the ones I have mentioned, but we need not spend our time with them now. Let us rather look at the words as they are here expounded by our Lord Himself. "I am going," He says. "What am I going to do? I am going to prepare a mansion for you."

> **D**o we in fact believe that the great goal that is confronting us is the goal of getting to the Father and getting to heaven? ∾

Do we in fact believe that the great goal that is confronting us is the goal of getting to the Father and getting to heaven? That is the question that the Gospel of Jesus Christ really does consider most; it is its one great central purpose. "But," says someone, "what I want to know is how I am to live in this world and how my world can be put in better order." Well, we may touch on that a little more in detail later, but I must report that there is no patent remedy in the New Testament Gospel for bringing about world peace; it does not promise us that.

The one thing the Gospel does promise us is eternal security in the matter of our ultimate destiny. It does not say, "Believe the Gospel and then you will never have any trouble in this life and world, and if you only believe it, it can banish war." Not at all! It is an utter travesty of the Gospel to believe that it does. Indeed men and women who believe that will be disillusioned, if they have not been disillusioned already. That kind of thing has been preached more in the last hundred years than it has ever been preached, and it is during that time that we have had two major world wars. So the Gospel's purpose is not to tell us how war can be avoided.

What it tells us is that whether there is another war or not, you and I are passing through this world of time. We have to die in any case, and the one thing that matters is how we can arrive at God and heaven and spend our eternity in the glory. That is what I am interested in, and that is the only thing that we should be interested in, because a day is coming when we will have no other interest and we shall be leaving the world and everything else behind. Then we shall be facing that unknown eternity and our great question, "How can I know God?", should have already been resolved by that time. As John Newton wrote,

And may the music of Thy name,
Refresh my soul in death.[1]

How then will that happen? Well, our Lord is dealing here with that precise thing. He does not merely say, "In my Father's house are many mansions." He adds, "I am here to tell you how you can get there." He makes a supremely logical proposition. It is something that He had to do for us and, blessed be His name, it is something that He has done for us. He does not turn to those men and say, "Look here, listen to me. I will tell you how you can arrive at that man-

---

1. Ed. note: From the hymn "How Sweet the Name of Jesus Sounds" by John Newton (1725-1807).

sion." He does not proceed to outline a programme of what we have to do in order that we may get to see God, and spend eternity in His presence in heaven. No, what He says is simply: "I am going to prepare that place for you."

> T*he Gospel is not an account of how you and I are to save ourselves.* ∾

Now this is the very beginning of the Gospel of Jesus Christ; it is an announcement and a proclamation of what the Son of God Himself has done for us. The Gospel is not an account of how you and I are to save ourselves, how we are to climb the steep ascent of heaven, and how we can obtain admission for ourselves. It starts by telling us that we can never do it, but it goes on to tell us that He has come deliberately into this world to do it for us. The only one who can ever admit us into heaven is the Lord Jesus Christ and what we have in these words is the beginning of His own exposition of the meaning of His death and Resurrection and Ascension.

"Now listen," he said to these men; "I am going to leave you, the time has come for the Son of Man to be glorified and God is glorified in Him." He was telling them that He was going to die; He was going to rise again from the grave and He was going to ascend into heaven. His objective was to make it possible for us to come with Him. Our entry into heaven, this entry into the eternal mansion and home with God, is something that is obtained for us by the Lord Jesus Christ, and by

Him alone. He has won our admission for us.

What, then, had He to do, in order to make that possible? Well, let us put it like this. What did he have to overcome for us that we could not overcome ourselves? The objective which we have in mind is admission into heaven and into the presence of God. But there are certain things which are standing between us and arriving there. Picture it to yourself, if you like, as a game of football.[2] There is a man with the ball at his feet. He wants to get to the goal but there are certain people trying to stop him. He has to get through and beyond them. You and I are in exactly the same position. Or think of it in a military way. There is a city which we want to enter but there are certain people standing, fully armed, trying to prevent our gaining an entrance. How can we get through?

Now what our Lord said to these men is what He says to us, that He was going ahead in order to clear the way and prepare a place for us. What are the things He had to do? I simply want to tabulate them in order that we may see something of the meaning of his glorious death. There are certain things here on earth, and certain things in heaven, that have to be done, before you and I can enter into the presence of God and enjoy the glory of eternity.

The first thing we encounter is the law of God. God not only made men and women, He gave them His laws, through which He told them how they were to live. He told them that it was only as they kept those laws that they could come into His presence and have fellowship with Him. Therefore, if I want to get to

2. Ed. note: "Football" is the British term for soccer.

heaven I am confronted by that legal demand. God says that unless you have honoured and kept all the law there is no admission for you into the presence of God. What is in God's law? The Ten Commandments are part of it, perhaps we need not go any further. I must worship God, and God alone; I must honour Him and no other. I must not worship any idol; not only idols made of wood and stone, but also idols such as myself or my profession or my money or my loved ones or my home. I must honour God's Sabbath day. I must not steal. I must not commit adultery. All of these commandments are the law of God. The Lord Jesus Christ summed it all up on one occasion when He said that this is the law of God: "Thou shalt love the Lord thy God with all thy heart, and with all thy soul, and with all thy strength, and with all thy mind; and thy neighbour as thyself" (Lk 10:27).

God's law is demanding of me, "Have you kept me? Have you honoured me?" If you have not, you cannot come into the presence of God. I have to face that fact whether I like it or not. Ignorance of the law is no excuse, is it? If you break the law of England, you are arrested and taken into court, but if you claim that you were not aware of the fact that there was such a law, do you think that the authorities will release you? If you think you are going to get away with it, you are making a big mistake! There is the law and it must be honoured.

Can we do it? I have never met a person who could, although many have tried. The other thing that confronts us is that because we have not kept and honoured the law, we are guilty before God and we are under the condemnation of the law because we have broken it. Is there anyone, I wonder, who does not feel guilty in the sight of God? Of course we all meet foolish people who tell us, "I do not feel I am a sinner," but what they mean by that is that they have never committed certain sins. We are all sinners. To be a sinner means that you have not given God all the honour and glory that are His due. *All* the glory. Indeed, however good and however moral we may be, to be living a self-righteous life is the depth of sin. So we are confronted by our own guilt and the condemnation of the law.

> To be a sinner means that you have not given God all the honour and glory that are His due. ∾

What else? Well, according to the Scripture the law pronounces that the punishment of sin is death, and death is right there demanding his dues. He says that men and women are sinners, they have sinned against God; "I demand them," he says, and he takes them unless, somehow or other, he can be dealt with. Death is a powerful enemy I have to face if I want to get to heaven. "The wages of sin is death" (Rom 6:23). That is why, as the author of the Epistle to the Hebrews puts it, we all of us, in a sense, spend our lifetime in the fear of death (Heb 2:15), because we have a horrible feeling that death is going to take hold of us and keep us from God.

Then the last enemy that we have to face is the devil, because, again, it is the teaching of Scripture that, as the result of man's sin, he has put himself under the power of the devil. And it is the devil who wields the power of death as we see in Hebrews 2:14. The devil is ready, as it were, to hurl us into death, and into the grip of hell, because we have come under his domination. He is there, standing in the pathway of anyone who tries, unaided, to arrive at God and to arrive in heaven at that mansion which is with God.

> God is light and in Him is no darkness at all... nothing impure or unworthy or sinful can enter into His presence. So... how can a man or woman enter into heaven without polluting it?

So there are these enemies and obstacles which we have to meet, whether we like it or not. We cannot avoid them, we have to face facts. But you know, there is an obstacle—I say it with reverence—even in heaven itself; God's own holiness and justice and righteousness. God is light and in Him is no darkness at all; He is absolutely pure and nothing impure or unworthy or sinful can enter into His presence. So the problem is this: how can a man or woman enter into heaven without polluting it? That is the problem which has to be met. How can God, in the words of Paul to the Romans, be just and yet a justifier of the ungodly (Rom 3:26)? And the ultimate problem is that even though somehow my sins were forgiven, how could I bear to stand in the presence of such a God?

Have you ever thought of that? You know what it is; we have all had the experience here on earth of being in the presence of some particularly good and saintly person. How unworthy it makes us feel; we feel uncomfortable in their presence because they are so good. Any special occasion, too, makes us feel nervous because of the greatness of the occasion. Multiply that by infinity and then see yourself standing in the presence of God. The Bible tells us of certain people who had a vision of God. Isaiah, for instance, said, "I am a man of unclean lips" (Is 6:5), while others went and hid themselves. The glory, the magnificence and the holiness of God was such that they felt it was almost insupportable.

Again, have you ever thought of that? I, just as I am now, am to be taken into heaven and the presence of this eternal God. But first something must be done to me! Something must happen to me to hide the rags even of my righteousness so that I can stand unashamed in heaven and, beyond that, enjoy and look at God. People tell me they find it very difficult at times to enjoy reading their Bible; they find it boring. They find prayer, too, and prayer meetings and listening to sermons about our Lord Jesus Christ rather boring. *If you are like that now, how do you think you can tolerate heaven?* In heaven they do nothing but praise God and worship Him and glorify Him and magnify His name. They talk about nothing else. They do not talk of things that interest people here on earth; none of them are mentioned. So how are you going to enjoy heaven?

*I*n heaven they do nothing but praise God and worship Him and glorify Him and magnify His name.... are you going to enjoy heaven? ～

Do you not see that something must happen to us? A lot of preparation is necessary before I can get to heaven. I thank God because He tells me, "I go to prepare a place for you." He has done it. He has answered every one of these demands. He has dealt with every enemy standing there sword in hand. He has dealt with every one of them and the way is wide open for me. He has lived the law of God perfectly; He has satisfied its every demand. He has kept the Ten Commandments and the whole of the moral law; He has pleased God in every detail and is absolutely satisfactory in His eyes. And He has done it as my representative. So the first enemy has been conquered.

And then I come to my guilt and condemnation under the law and, thank God, Christ has vanquished this also. He has taken upon Himself the responsibility of my guilt and my failure and my utter condemnation by making Himself an offering to God. He has presented Himself as a sacrifice and God has "laid upon Him the iniquity of us all" (Is 53:6). Your guilt and mine has been transferred to Him and it has been dealt with—that second enemy has been conquered.

But then He goes on to meet the next enemy, for to

meet the demands of the law, you see, He inevitably had to meet death. As I have reminded you, "the wages of sin is death." The pronouncement of the law was that anyone who failed to keep the law should die, and He faced the demand of death. Death says "I claim these people as the result of sin," so Christ had to meet death. He paid the required price.

*C*hrist had to meet death. ∾

Death thought it had conquered Him, for He died and was buried in a grave, and death seemed to be victorious. But wait a minute! The morning of the third day arrived and He burst asunder the bands of death and arose "triumphant o'er the grave." Thus Paul, in addressing the church at Corinth, can say, "Death is swallowed up in victory. O death, where is thy sting? O grave, where is thy victory?" (1 Cor 15:54-55). Behold Him, then, risen; the last enemy that shall be conquered is death and it has been conquered.

But there I see still an enemy, this foul angelic being called the devil, who has consigned so many to death and to hell. He still waits and claims his power and tries to exercise his tyranny. He says to me, "Yes, though you believe all that, I still accuse you." But again I have my answer for him: "Forasmuch then as the children are partakers of flesh and blood, he also himself likewise took part of the same; that through death he might destroy him that had the power of death, that is, the devil; And deliver them who through fear of death were all their lifetime subject to bondage" (Heb 2:14-15). He met the devil in single mortal combat many times here on earth, and He defeated Him every time. The devil came to Him during the forty days in the wilderness and He defeated him there. He defeated him in the Garden of Gethsemane. Again He destroyed him on the Cross when all hell was let loose against Him. He defeated and conquered the devil.

> *All these enemies, therefore, that stood against me this side of heaven have been met and defeated.* ∽

All these enemies, therefore, that stood against me this side of heaven have been met and defeated. He has opened the way. So I am at the door and gateway of heaven, but, alas, I am faced with the justice and the righteousness and the holiness of God! But it is all right; He has even dealt with that. God Himself "was in Christ, reconciling the world unto himself" (2 Cor 5:19), and the justice and the righteousness of God have been satisfied by Christ's reconciling sacrifice. Punishment of sin has been meted out on Jesus instead of on us. What man deserved has been cast upon Him. It is true that God can be just and the justifier of the ungodly at one and the same time.

There is a most amazing statement made about this in the ninth chapter of Hebrews. "You remember," the writer says, in effect, "that in the old dispensation, the earthly temple had to be purified with the blood of bulls and of goats. But, you know," he says, "that is not good enough for the heavenly tabernacle. The heavenly temple itself needs to be purified and nothing but the blood of Christ can purify the heavenly things themselves." What he means is that the blood of Christ is so efficacious that I can go into heaven without polluting it (Heb 9:18-28). His blood purifies it in that sense and it also does it by reconciling the justice and the love, the righteousness and the mercy of God. So heaven is clear and the way is open.

And then, of course, He does all this by giving me His own righteousness. So when I come to enter there, God will not see me as I am; He will see me clothed with the righteousness of Jesus Christ. I am in Christ, and I am covered by Him and His spotless perfect life. I have everything I need—"I go to prepare a place for you"; no one else could have done it, but, blessed be His holy name, He has done it. Every obstacle has been removed and the door of heaven is open for me, even me.

Consider, finally, what it meant to Him to do this for us. "I go," He says. Where is He going? He is going to the Garden of Gethsemane to sweat drops of blood. Where is He going? He is going to be arrested, to be tried in court, to be mocked and jeered and laughed at. He is going to be spat upon, to have His holy body scourged. He is going to have a crown of thorns placed upon His head. They will take Him and drive cruel nails into His blessed hands and feet. He is going to be nailed to a tree. Can you picture it happening to you, with nails being hammered in through hands and feet? That is what He is going to. And, too,

He is going to endure the mockery and the spitting and the jeering of the cruel mob; they did not know who He was or what He was doing. He is going to die and to be laid in a grave, He who is the eternal Son of God through whom the world was made and by whom all things consist. He is going deliberately to all that because that is the only way whereby the door and the gate of heaven can be opened for us. "I go to prepare a place in heaven with God, a mansion for you."

Beloved friend, have you realised that the Lord Jesus Christ has done all that for you? If you see it, if you believe it, you will agree with Paul when he says that you are not your own, you "are bought with a price," therefore you must give yourself and your life to Him (1 Cor 6:20). If you believe Him, you can know for certain that He has prepared a place for you and will come again and receive you unto Himself so that where He is, you shall be also.

SIX

"I Will Come Again, and Receive You"

> "Men of Galilee, why stand ye gazing up into heaven? this same Jesus, which is taken up from you into heaven, shall so come in like manner as ye have seen him go into heaven."
>
> **Acts 1:11**

THERE ARE, AS WE HAVE SEEN, certain requirements that have to be met before we can ever arrive in that mansion which is prepared for us in our Father's house, and we have considered how our Lord met them. We saw how He met and looked at the law's demands, how He met the devil, how He met death and hell and how He faced even the problem of the holiness of God Himself. And in that amazing phrase of the author of the Epistle to the Hebrews, we saw how He even purified the heavenly places in order to ensure that our entrance does not introduce pollution. So we are free to enjoy the blessings that await us in that mansion.

So we come now to the next step. "If I go and prepare a place for you, I will come again, and receive you unto myself; that where I am, there ye may be also" (Jn 14:3). "It is all right," says our Lord in effect, "because I will come back and I will take you and receive you unto myself, so that you are not going to lose me; you are going to be with me throughout the countless ages of eternity."

Now it is generally agreed that this statement is a reference to what is commonly called the *Second Coming* of the Lord Jesus Christ. It may, in addition, have various other meanings about how our Lord comes to us spiritually and so on, and yet I think that obviously its main meaning is that of the Second Coming, one of the critical doctrines of the Christian faith; one of the great central doctrines of this New Testament teaching and, therefore, a doctrine which of necessity we must consider together.

Let me introduce this subject to you like this: I am coming increasingly to the conclusion that one of the best ways of testing whether men and women are Christians or not, whether they really do believe and live by the Christian faith, is not so much to ask them directly for their view of the Lord Jesus Christ, but rather to confront them with this particular doctrine. Instead of asking them, "What do you think of Christ?" or, "What is your view of the person of Jesus of Nazareth as it is displayed in the New Testament Gospels?" I think a much more certain and subtle way of discovering whether people really are Christians is to ask them leading questions such as these:

What is your view of what is happening in the world at the present time? How do you react to it? Are you surprised at it? Does the present state of the world and the prospects that seem to lie ahead of us fit into your philosophy of this life or do they not? Are you driven into the depths of despair by what is happening in the world today? Is it something that has come crashing into all your calculations and ideas, or is it something that fits naturally and inevitably into your view of life and of the whole course of history? What is your forecast of the future? What are you expecting of life? What are you anticipating in the realm of history?

Now people cannot answer those questions without telling you, very plainly and surely, whether they are Christians in the New Testament sense of that term or not. There is no more direct way of discovering that than by bringing people immediately face to face with the world situation and asking them their ultimate explanation. Alternatively, we can put it to them in terms of this extraordinary teaching of the New Testament with regard to the Second Coming of Christ.

In other words, does this doctrine of the Second Coming seem remote to you or quite irrelevant? Do you take the view that so many take? They say, "What I want from preachers is something that is going to help me to live in this world here and now. You are talking about something that is going to happen sometime, about the reappearance of the Son of God into this world. Now if you were preaching like that many years ago, when life was complacent and leisurely and when it was an interesting thing to debate these theological points, I would not have objected. But, surely, with the world as it is today, are you going to spend your time discussing these remote ideas?" Now if that is your position, you are displaying immediately your attitude toward the Christian Gospel.

D*oes this doctrine of the Second Coming seem remote to you or quite irrelevant?* ∾

Or let me put it like this. What is your view of Christianity and of its teaching? Is it that it is something which is to be applied to life, a great ethical and moral and social teaching which it is our business as men and women to apply to life and its circumstances? Do we believe that as the result of so doing we will improve the social conditions and the international situation, we will get rid of war and all sorts of trouble, and we will introduce the kingdom of God and make this world another paradise? Is that our view of it? Well, that has been the view of many people and of all those in the world today who are astonished and unhappy, these people are the ones who are most surprised.

But one is constantly meeting large numbers of people who believe this argument: "I cannot possibly become a Christian," they say. And when we ask them what their problem is, they reply, "My difficulty is this; you claim that your message is one which has been given by God to mankind. Well, that Gospel of yours has been preached now for nearly two thousand years and for a time it had the monopoly of the thoughts and minds of men, but look at the state of the world! If the Gospel of Jesus Christ is the thing that is going to put the world right, isn't it time it did so? So," they say, "I just cannot believe it." Now, there is only one thing to say to such people, and that is that they have an entirely erroneous view of what the Gospel of Jesus Christ really is.

So I want to put my message to you in terms of that kind of question. I am looking at the sort of people who really are quite sincere, and I want to show that such a question is nothing but a sheer misunderstanding of the teaching of the Gospel and what it promises. In their perplexity they regard the Gospel as something which is to be applied to life and, by its application, they think life can be reformed and improved. And so it follows that they often feel that this teaching of the Second Coming of Christ is so remote as to be finally irrelevant.

W*e must be perfectly clear about what the Gospel has to say about the world and its history. It tells us that life in this world... has been vitiated and ruined by sin.* ॐ

What, then, does the Gospel really teach?

Now here in this passage I suggest we have it in a nutshell. Our Lord is addressing men who are continuing to live in this world. He tells them that they will have troubles and trials and tribulations. What comfort has He to give them? You notice what He does? He talks about His death and the Cross, and then He goes straight from the death and the Resurrection to the Second Coming. Not a word, for the moment, about anything that intervenes in between. Haven't we noticed this before in the New Testament record?

So let us divide this up. First, we must be perfectly clear about what the Gospel really has to say about the world and its history. It tells us that life in this world and the whole history of the human race has gone radically wrong; it has been vitiated and ruined by sin.

Now that is, of course, as we must all agree, whatever our view may be, something which is quite fundamental. The whole teaching of the Bible, from beginning to end, is that the trouble with men and women, with life and with history, is radical. The real problem is sin. Sin is something that does not merely affect the surface of life; it affects the very source. And the result of all this is that the life of this world is under the control of sin, under the control of Satan.

B*iblical teaching is, quite categorically, that sin is such a radical problem that the world cannot now and never will improve itself.* ❧

Now some people today think that it is ignorant to believe in Satan. Well, if you feel like that, I just ask you to look at the world and at yourself and try to explain some of the things that happen, both within you, and in the world, apart from the biblical teaching about Satan and the hosts and powers of evil, these malign influences that are there unseen in the spiritual realm.

The next step in the argument is that the world, as it is in sin and under the control of Satan, cannot be improved. Indeed, I defy anyone to show that Scripture teaches that it can. Biblical teaching is, quite categorically, that sin is such a radical problem that the world cannot now and never will improve itself; there is no hope for it in that way. So we begin to see why the man or woman who is truly Christian, who bases all opinions on scriptural teaching, is not a bit surprised at what is happening in the world today.

Our Lord and Saviour Himself said, "As it was in the days of Noah, so shall it be also in the days of the Son of man.... Likewise also as it was in the days of Lot... " (Lk 17:26, 28). He spans the centuries; He lays down the proposition that because of sin and the fall, mankind *as mankind* is going to be not different at the end of history from what it was at the very beginning. There is nothing, therefore, which is such an utter travesty of the Christian Gospel as the suggestion that because it is being preached, each generation will be better than the previous one, and the world will reform and improve, until everything that is evil and wrong will have been banished and ultimately all will be perfect.

The Gospel never teaches that, it asserts the exact opposite. I do not apologise for saying that the Bible's view of history is profoundly pessimistic. Of course, that is why the Bible is not very popular and has not been so during the last hundred years. Evolutionary theories and hypotheses are very optimistic; they all tell us that the world is going to be better and better and that mankind is evolving and advancing. Philosophers always want to be optimistic if they can be and thus they paint this picture of improvement. And, of course, if you believe them, you cannot like the Bible, because its realism contrasts sharply with these optimistic ideas.

It was Christ Himself who said, "There shall be wars and rumours of wars" (Mt 24:6). His teaching was that while lusts and passions and greed and jealousy and envy are in the human heart, wars will continue. You see, the Bible is not foolish enough to think you can have one thing on the personal level and another on the international level. As long as two people fight and quarrel, nations will do the same, and they are doing so, in spite of all the fatal belief in the effect of education and international conferences to make men wise.

> A*s long as two people fight and quarrel, nations will do the same... in spite of the effect of education and international conferences to make men wise.* ∾

No, what is in the heart of man will express itself. We all know that the tendency in all people is to fight. The cause is sin, this terrible, malign power in the human race that drives us to self-destruction. The state of the world reflects the state of sin which dominates our lives; this is the biblical message. Furthermore, the Bible goes on to tell us that, as a result of all this, the world is under judgement, that the whole of human history is moving to a grand and ultimate climax, that God, because He is God and because He is what He is, has pronounced His judgement upon sin and evil and wrong. That judgement will finally be executed at the end.

So that is the first principle. The second is that the Bible not only says things like that about the world and human history; it also has something to tell us about God's redeeming purpose in history or what you may describe as a kind of divine history. The world is as it is because of man's disobedience and sin, but, thank God, He has not left it at that. There is a description of the state of the world in the Bible, as we have seen, but it does not stop at description; the whole point is to tell us what God has done about it.

> T*he world is as it is because of man's disobedience and sin, but, thank God, He has not left it at that.* ❧

What, then, is God's purpose? Again I start with the same negative. His plan and purpose is not to reform that world but to take and save the people out of it. God's purpose is to take hold of individuals and to put them into another kingdom which is His kingdom and the kingdom of His dear Son. The very person who uttered these words which we are considering is none other than God's only begotten Son, the one whom God has sent into this world to bring this gracious purpose to pass. When He was on earth He chose various ways to say to the people, "The world is perishing; but come to me and become a member of my kingdom and you will be delivered, saved from the wrath of God." He has come, as Paul says to the Galatians, "to deliver us from this present evil world" (Gal 1:4), to rescue us out of the dominion of Satan.

We have already touched on this in passing, but the effect of the Gospel is to enable us to see the nature of life in this world and to bring us to see that what really matters for us is our soul, that our greatest concern should not even be the possibility of a third world war.

> *If I have not awakened to the fact that my soul and my relationship to God are infinitely more important than the possibility that my body may be destroyed by a nuclear bomb, then I have not started to be a Christian.* ℘

Now I am not denouncing politics, nor the international efforts to ensure peace. That is not my purpose. What I do maintain is that if I have not awakened to the fact that my soul and my relationship to God are infinitely more important than the possibility that my body may be destroyed by a nuclear bomb, then I have not started to be a Christian. I must realise that it is my soul, my eternal destiny, my relationship to God that matters. The effect of the Gospel upon men and women is to bring them to see themselves as strangers in this world of time. They sit loosely to time and the things that happen in this world, and see themselves as pilgrims bound for eternity—that is the big, the thrilling thing.

The business of the Gospel of Jesus Christ, therefore, is not either to reform the individual or the whole world, it is to take hold of us one by one and to bring us out of it; to give us a new birth, a new life, a new beginning. It makes men and women children of God; it gives them a new outlook, a new power, and sets before them that blessed hope of life with God in eternity.

That, let me emphasise again, is the Christian message. The Gospel is not merely an exposition of the Sermon on the Mount and its social application, in order to make a better place of this world. Men have been preaching that kind of thing for so many years and trying to put it into practice. But look at the results! To ask unregenerate people to live the Sermon on the Mount is mockery; they cannot do it. They cannot even keep the Ten Commandments; they cannot live to their own moral standards. But how glibly people talk about "the social application of the Gospel," and about bringing in the kingdom of God.

There is a kingdom of darkness and a kingdom of light, and these two kingdoms are here together in this world. ❧

Oh! the tragedy of it all! No, we need to be born again, to be regenerated, and the Gospel offers to do that. So that, side by side in this world of time, you have these new people, the citizens of the kingdom of God, and those who belong to Satan. "Ye," said Christ to the Pharisees, "are of your father the devil, and the lusts of your father ye will do" (Jn 8:44). There is a kingdom of darkness and a kingdom of light, and these two kingdoms are here together in this world—that is another aspect of the Gospel message.

Then the next principle is this. Ultimately these two histories, these two kingdoms will meet and then there will be an end. That is the essence of the doctrine of the Second Coming of Christ. This New Testament Gospel tells us that as certainly as the Son of God came into this world as the babe of Bethlehem, as certainly as His disciples lived with Him and saw Him ascend into the heavens, so He will return again into this world, visibly, in a bodily form. This is the statement; you get it in every epistle. As Peter reminds us, the Lord Himself said it (2 Pt 3:13), the first apostles all preached it, but nobody believed it. The world has never believed this kind of message. But here it is and it is a part of Christian preaching to proclaim it.

Now I am not going to deal now with the various ramifications and theories and ideas about the details of this Second Coming of Christ, to me that is not the important matter. The important matter is to grasp this great central statement that He is coming again and that He is coming to judge. The world and its peoples, all who have ever lived, will be judged. There is to be a final assize. Everything that is evil and belongs to Satan and his kingdom will be destroyed; it will be cast into the lake of destruction and fire. And, as Peter put it, there will be "new heavens and a new earth, wherein dwelleth righteousness" (2 Pt 3:13). Everything sinful and tarnishing will be purged out of the universe and there is to be a new world, in which there will be absolute righteousness.

And—you can be very sure of this—all who belong to the Lord Jesus Christ; who have seen the all-importance of the soul; who have seen their dread condition under the condemnation of the law; who have believed in Christ and His sacrificial death; who have committed themselves to Him, taking upon themselves the scorn and sarcasm of the world; those who have counted all things loss for his sake, who have denied themselves and taken up their cross daily and followed Him; those who have said, "I care not what happens to me as long as all is well between me and Him"—these are they who will be with Him in the new heaven and the new earth and will share and enjoy His glory for ever and ever.

> *Those who have said, "I care not what happens to me as long as all is well between me and Him"... will share and enjoy His glory for ever and ever.* ❧

"When is this Second Coming going to happen?" asks someone. And the answer is, I do not know and nobody else knows. We are not to be concerned with times and seasons but we should be tremendously concerned about the event. If you are Christians, said

Peter to those early Christians, you will be looking for these things and hastening their coming (2 Pt 3:12). You will realise that this is the one thing that matters and you will look forward to it. You will expect it; you will prepare yourself for it; you will realise what sort of a person you ought to be in the light of it.

People are so concerned to try to fix times and seasons. There are those who tell us that the Second Coming may be very near. And there are people throughout the centuries, as Peter reminds us, who have scoffed at the idea and have said, "Where is the promise of his coming?" (2 Pt 3:4). This Gospel has been preached for nearly two thousand years, they say today, but He hasn't come again yet. Yes, and they spoke like that before the Flood! People have always done that sort of thing and when the Son of God came into the world the first time, it did not even recognise Him. Remember: "One day is with the Lord as a thousand years, and a thousand years as one day" (2 Pt 3:8). I ask you again, face the facts; look at the world situation and try to explain it in any other terms than I have used. Do you not see that man, in his malignity, his enmity against God, and his foolishness, is just fulfilling Scripture and its prophecies? And above all, I ask you to see yourself involved in all this.

Finally, what is the promise to the Christian in the light of all this? Let me remind you of it and it is the thing that is most urgent for all of us. I do not want to be pessimistic, I do not know exactly what is going to happen in the world, but I do know that whatever may happen, everyone of us has got to die and to leave this world. And what have I to say about that? Well, death to Christian men and women, to those who have believed on the Lord Jesus Christ, means that they go to be with Christ. It is His promise to us. He said to that thief dying at His side on the Cross, "Today shalt thou be with me in paradise" (Lk 23:43).

There are those who would say that one of the things which He had in mind when He said, "I will come again, and receive you unto myself," was just that; that as you and I come to die, it will not be lonely, it will not be terrible, it will not be going to some great unknown. No, He will be there. I am not sure that that is straight from Scripture, but I am entitled to say this. He said Himself about the poor beggar Lazarus that when he died he was "carried by the angels into Abraham's bosom" (Lk 16:22). That is the death of a believer; it is not horrible; the angels of God will be there to receive you and to carry you to Him. I am quoting the apostle Paul when I say that "to die is gain," for it means "to be with Christ; which is far better" (Phil 1:21, 23).

> *As you and I come to die, it will not be lonely, it will not be terrible, it will not be going to some great unknown. No, He will be there.* ❧

The Bible does not give us many details at that point, I do not suppose we could stand them if we were given them; the thing is too tremendous; it is too glorious for us to think of. But of this I am certain,

that when He comes again there will be a general resurrection. All shall rise; those who remain on earth
when He comes will "be changed, in a moment, in the
twinkling of an eye" (1 Cor 15:51-52). There will be a
great resurrection and what our Lord tells me is that I
shall be prepared for that new order, for that new
earth, under those new heavens, even by receiving a
changed body. This body of my humiliation shall be
changed. There will be no disease then, because we
shall not be stricken with diseases and infirmities. We
shall be "fashioned like unto his glorious body" (Phil
3:21). We shall be like Him, we shall see Him, we shall
be transmuted and glorified like Him and enjoy that
bliss and those blessings with Him for ever and for
ever.

That is the comfort to those who believe on Him.
"Let not your heart be troubled"; do not feel all is lost,
because Jesus tells us, "I go to prepare a place for you.
And if I go and prepare a place for you, I will come
again and receive you unto myself; that where I am,
there ye may be also." I believe that I, miserable sinner
such as I am, am nevertheless going to look into the
blessed face of the Son of God and be like Him and
spend eternity in His holy, glorious, loving presence.
This is true about any person who believes on the Lord
Jesus Christ as the Son of God. If you believe that He
died for your sins and rose again to justify you, if you
give yourself to Him and live for Him, that will happen
to you.

"Beloved, now are we the sons of God, and it doth
not yet appear what we shall be: but we know that,

when he shall appear, we shall be like him; for we shall see him as he is" (1 Jn 3:2). I suggest to you that, in the midst of the darkness and the confusion and the uncertainty of this modern world, if you want rest, if you want peace, if you want quietness of heart, you will not find it by trusting to ideas as to the reformation of this world, for these are all being falsified before your eyes. No, you will find peace only there where you will find this assurance that whatever may happen to you in this world of time, nothing, nothing, shall be able to separate you from the love of God which is in Christ Jesus our Lord and the glory of being with Him for ever and ever.

Do you know it? Do you believe it? Give yourself no rest or peace until you have that blessed assurance.

PART III
No Other Way

∾

"I am the way, the truth and the life:
no man cometh unto the Father, but by me.
If ye had known me, ye should have
known my Father also: and from henceforth
ye know him, and have seen him....
Verily, verily, I say unto you, he that believeth
on me, the works that I do shall he do also;
and greater works than these shall he do;
because I go unto my Father."
JOHN 14:6-7, 12

SEVEN

"I Am the Way, the Truth, and the Life"

∾

And because ye are sons, God hath sent forth
the Spirit of his Son into your hearts,
crying, "Abba, Father."
Galatians 4:6

"I AM THE WAY, THE TRUTH, AND THE LIFE: no man cometh unto the Father, but by me" (Jn 14:6). In this verse we find again one of those summaries of the central truth of the Christian Gospel. Of course in many ways it is nothing but a summary of everything that our Lord had already been saying to the disciples, but it became necessary for Him to repeat it and to summarise it all again, because of the question put by the apostle Thomas.

Now let me remind you, once more, of the setting. If we are truly to understand and grasp this momentous statement, we must bear that in mind. Here is our Lord about to go to His death on the Cross and He informs His followers that He is about to leave them, and, naturally, they become crestfallen and unhappy.

So He, recognising this, administers to them this wonderful comfort. "Let not your heart be troubled," He says, "… believe in God, believe also in me." And then he outlines the great purpose which He is going to fulfil by going to His death, to His Resurrection, to His Ascension and to everything that follows. "Do not be troubled," He says, "do not be disturbed or unhappy, do not regard my departure as being the end of all things. It is not, it is far from that; in a sense it is only the beginning. 'I go to prepare a place for you,' that is why I am going and I am going deliberately." In other words, he confronts them with the great promise of the Christian Gospel; it is His way of presenting to them the whole scheme and plan and way of salvation. "It is all right," He says, "I am going to leave you and you will not see me with the naked eye; but I am going to the Father and I am going to prepare a place for you with the Father. I am going to make ready for you that mansion that is there awaiting you with the Father, and, when the time comes, I will come back and receive you, and all others who believe on me, unto myself, so that where I am, there you may be also."

We have been considering all that in detail. We have looked together at the purpose of Jesus' death on the Cross, the whole purpose of the Resurrection, the Ascension, and what our Lord has even done for us in heaven. And then we have looked at that mighty statement about His coming back again, about the Second Coming of Christ, the final end of history, the consummation of the age, the final judgement, the

destruction of sin and evil and all that belong to it and
the ushering in of the glorious kingdom of God, the
reign of Christ and the glory of the saints.

So our Lord has been putting all that to these men,
and He sums it all up by saying, "'Whither I go ye
know'—you have been with me now for nearly three
years and you are familiar with my teaching. Therefore,
you know where I am going and you know the way I
am going. You know that the way ultimately will lead
you to be with me in glory." In effect, he turns to
them and says, "Therefore, all you have to do now is
to follow me. I have told you the plan, I have outlined
to you the purpose. I have tried to make you see that I
am going in order to prepare this glorious, wonderful
prospect for you. So you are quite clear about it all—
where I am going and the way to get there."

And then Thomas speaks, Thomas with his little
faith. Thomas, who is perhaps still thinking in Jewish
and in materialistic terms about the kingdom, does not
understand this. What is our Lord really saying? "Is he
saying," thinks Thomas, "that He is just going to dis-
appear for a little while and that then He will come
back fairly quickly in order to establish His kingdom
among us? Is He coming back after a while to deliver
us from the Roman bondage and tyranny and set us
free in a military and political sense? Is that it?"

"I do not understand this," Thomas says. "You say,
'Whither I go ye know, and the way ye know.' Well, I
am sorry, but I do not know. Lord, we know not
whither thou goest; and how can we know the way?

The thing is a mystery to me. I do not know what you mean by going to prepare a place, and so on, and that you are coming again."

T*homas stumbles.... we should be very grateful to him for his sterling honesty in expressing himself so frankly and plainly.* ॐ

Thomas stumbles; probably he is blinded by his prejudices, so he speaks and makes his double protest. And we should be very grateful to him for his sterling honesty in expressing himself so frankly and plainly. We have benefitted from other glimpses of this man Thomas in the Gospels. They are all of a pattern. A plain man, rather a blunt man, and yet, to me at any rate, a very loveable man. He was a man whose heart, it seems, was, generally speaking, better than his mind. You remember that when our Lord was proposing to go to the house of Lazarus who was desperately ill, Thomas thought it was an awful mistake. He said, "Let us also go, that we may die with Him" (Jn 11:16). That is the sort of man he was.

Even after the Resurrection, he could not quite follow it. The death of our Lord upon the Cross had been a shattering blow to Thomas in spite of all this preparation. Evidently he had gone home and the result was that when our Lord appeared in the Upper Room to the disciples, Thomas was not there. Then he came back; he was not happy. Though he was slow to understand, there was a ferment working in him and he felt drawn back to the others. So he went back to them. But when they said to him, "The Lord has been amongst us," Thomas said, "I won't believe it, until I can put my finger into the print of the nails, and thrust my hand into His side, I cannot believe it until I have actually seen for myself." Then, you remember, our Lord came again and said, "Thomas, reach hither thy finger, and behold my hands; and reach hither thy hand, and thrust it into my side: and be not faithless, but believing." And Thomas fell at His feet and said, "My Lord and my God" (Jn 20:27-28).

So let us thank God for the honesty of Thomas, because it was his question that led our Lord to make this momentous statement that we are considering. Thomas has a double difficulty and our Lord deals with it by making a double reply. "Lord," says Thomas, "we know not wither thou goest; and how can we know the way?"

"Very well," said Christ to him, "I am the way, the truth, and the life: no man cometh unto the Father," —that is the destination—"but by me."

Now all this is not only of interest to us in terms of Thomas and those first disciples, it is the most urgent and relevant question for us today. We are confronted by this great statement; Christ still speaks to us down the ages and He says to us in our troubled and unhappy modern world— "Let not your heart be troubled." That is the great pronouncement of the Gospel; you need not be troubled if you only believe this message.

But oh, many of us are like this man Thomas. We say, "What is all this? We do not understand; what is it trying to say to us?" Well, the Gospel comes right down to meet us. Thank God for the honesty of the Gospel writers also, that they did not hesitate to put in these human difficulties. The Gospel does not hesitate to report that Thomas was in difficulty and expressing his scepticism. So here our Lord amplifies His statement and summarises, for Thomas and for us, the two vital and most essential points. And it is to these two great points I want to direct your attention now.

M*any of us are like this man Thomas.* ❧

The first thing we must be clear about is the destination. What is the goal? What is it that mankind really needs in an ultimate sense? And this is our Lord's answer: our destination is God, and the knowledge of God as Father. That is what we need; that is what we should be setting out for, that is our destiny. "We know not whither thou goest," says Thomas. "Well," says our Lord in reply, "I am going to the Father and no man comes to the Father but by me. That is the destiny; that is the place I am going to. I am going to the Father and you must follow me to Him; and what you must ultimately be concerned about is that you yourself should arrive there." Later he puts it still more clearly, "If ye had known me, ye should have known my Father also: and from henceforth ye know him, and have seen him" (Jn 14:7).

I can go on and point out to you that Philip, the other apostle, by putting his question also at this point, really emphasised and underlined the same thing. The moment our Lord said that, Philip said, "Lord, shew us the Father, and it sufficeth us" (v. 8), and Jesus said to him, "Have I been so long time with you, and yet hast thou not known me, Philip? he that hath seen me hath seen the Father; and how sayest thou *then*, Shew us the Father? Believest thou not that I am in the Father, and the Father in me?" (vv. 9-10).

There, then, is the first point which we must grasp and understand. Here we are, living in this world with all its difficulties and its trials, its pain and its contradictions, and we are like these men Thomas and Philip. We want to know where we are going, what is it we really need. And that is the answer. Our ultimate need and desire is the knowledge of God, and especially this knowledge of God as Father. Philip, I think, puts it very well for us all—"Show us the Father, and it sufficeth us."

T*he greatest need of any person is to know God, to arrive at God.* ॐ

Now I want to unfold that statement a little with you. The greatest need of any person is to know God, to arrive at God. If we are not clear about that, we are not clear about the thing that you and I need if we want to know rest and peace and a quiet heart.

"Knowing God" does not mean only that we should believe certain things about God, nor merely that we should believe in the being and existence of God. I do not mean only that we should believe that He is the creator, the maker and the sustainer of all things.

> *I can know God, not as someone who is far away in the distance, of whom I am frightened... but I can turn to Him and trust Him as my Father.* ∾

No, what the Bible, and especially the New Testament, offers us is an actual knowledge of God. We are to know Him as our Father. "No man," says Christ, "cometh unto the Father, but by me," so that I can know God, not as someone who is far away in the distance, of whom I am frightened, a tyrannical someone who is set against me, but I can turn to Him and trust Him as my Father. "Ye have received the Spirit of adoption," says the apostle Paul, "whereby we cry, Abba, Father" (Rom 8:15). In other words, we realise that God is someone who loves us with an everlasting love, that He is so concerned about us that the very hairs of our head are all numbered and that nothing can happen to us apart from God and outside His will.

This knowledge of God about which our Lord is here speaking, means that we have fellowship with God. This same writer, the apostle John, in his first epistle, (written when John was an old man) tells the Christians to whom he is writing that his great object is that their joy—even in this world of time—might be full (1 Jn 1:4). Indeed the setting is very similar to our

Lord's many years before. He was leaving His disciples and He wanted to give them comfort before He left. Now here is an elderly John, one of those apostles, writing to the Christians and saying, "Before I go, I want to give you some joy and happiness even in a world like this. I want you," he says, "to have 'fellowship with us: and truly our fellowship is with the Father, and with His Son Jesus Christ'" (1 Jn 1:3).

Now this is the central thing that is offered us by the New Testament Gospel; I can put it best of all at this point in the form of some questions: What exactly is your relationship to God? Can you say that you *know* God? Is He real to you? Is He personal to you? When you say your prayers, are you conscious that God is there and that He is listening to you? Have you got a filial affection with respect to God in your heart? Do you know for certain that you are in contact and in communion with Him? When you turn to Him in prayer about any question whatsoever, do you do so with confidence? Do you feel that the access is free and easy, that it is open and that you really are speaking to God in that personal sense?

If you can say "yes," then you know what I mean by fellowship with God. It is the very thing about which our Lord was speaking to these disciples before He left them. Come to the Father; yes, come to the Father even while we are in this world, having that certain knowledge of Him and that intimacy with Him, so that whatever may happen to us in this life, we are always in touch with God and always in communion and fellowship with Him.

*When illness comes, or accident or
war or trial or persecution, or
even death itself, I can immediately
speak to God and know that I am in
His hand.* ❧

In other words, it should be that we are able to say,
as the Bible says we should, "The Lord is my helper,
and I will not fear what man shall do unto me" (Heb
13:6). So that when illness comes, or accident or war
or trial or persecution, or even death itself, I can immediately speak to God and know that I am in His hand.
So that whatever happens to me, I know "all things
work together for good to them that love God" (Rom
8:28). Come to the Father—really come to know God,
so that God becomes to you more real, in a sense, than
anything you see. This is essential to the obtaining of a
quiet and untroubled heart.

We must also know that we are to be with God at
the end of the journey and in eternity. The *summum
bonum* of all Christian living is to see God—"Blessed
are the pure in heart, for they shall see God" (Mt 5:8).
We have been considering that. Let me emphasise
again that the most important thing that we can ever
know in this world is that a day is coming when we
shall stand in the presence of God and share His glory
for ever and ever, to spend our eternity with Him,
knowing Him, communing with Him. We know and
trust Him now, while we go on through this journey
which we call life, and then, at the end, we will stand
before Him and hear Him say, "Well done, good and

faithful servant.... Enter thou into the joy of thy lord"
(Mt 25:23). That is the destination and that is the
great purpose.

So the answer to Thomas' statement about his not
knowing where he was going is that he was going to
the Father. And it is still the answer to every doubting
Thomas. The Christian message is not about international relations or world peace; no, the central matter of the Gospel is that we should know God and
enjoy Him for all eternity.

> *Christians start with the ultimate
> and eternal and then they come
> back to the present.* ∾

Of course, let me emphasise again that does not
mean that we are indifferent to the world. I am not
saying that because we are Christians we should not be
concerned about the state of the world. But I do say
that if we fix our attention only upon this world and
this life, we are not taking the Christian view.

Christians start with the ultimate and eternal and
then they come back to the present. And those who
have not prepared for the ultimate before they face the
present are living in a fool's paradise. Whatever may
happen in this world, this year or next year or any
other year, even if hell be let loose, if you know God as
your Father, you need not be afraid of anything.
Whatever happens you are safe and your destiny is
guaranteed if you are a child of God.

That, then, was Thomas' difficulty about the desti-

142

nation. Now let us look at his second difficulty, which was how to get to the destination. "Well," says Christ, "the simple answer for Thomas is this: I am the way." Now you notice that, again, He does not merely talk or teach about the way, or give instruction as to how Thomas may find it. His claim is, "I myself am the way." He does not even leave it at that. He goes on to say that He is the *only* way to the Father; "No man," he says, "cometh unto the Father but by me," or "through me." Now this again is a momentous statement. We must face it. Let me put it, therefore, as a blunt assertion. This Jesus of Nazareth, who here speaks these words, is absolutely essential and vital. There is no knowledge of God apart from Him, there is no communion with God apart from Him; He says categorically, "… *but by me.*"

Now I emphasise this because I think nothing is more tragic than the way in which so many people still seem to fail to realise the absolute centrality and necessity of the Lord Jesus Christ. I recently read a book which purports to help men and women to try to find God and this quiet heart; but as I read it, I saw very clearly that Christ was not emphasised as essential. Yet here He is telling us Himself that no man or woman can ever come to a knowledge of God as Father unless they come through Him and by Him.

Someone once described a marvellous experience of God which came to him as he listened to a performance of a Beethoven symphony. He said that as he listened to the entrancing music, he had this experience and he came to know God. Well, all I would say to that is that unless that experience led that man to see the absolute centrality of the Lord Jesus Christ, then he is suffering from a delusion; he has had no experience of God. Unless this Christ, the Son of God, is in the central place as the *way* to God, there is no Gospel.

Let us be clear about this—there are counterfeit experiences. Certainly the man experienced something as he listened to the symphony concert. But the question is, was it an experience of God? Certainly people have felt a curious uplift of the spirit perhaps as they have seen a glorious sunset or as they have read some magnificent piece of poetry. You can read of strange and marvellous experiences that many people claim to have received. There are people who will tell you that in your troubles and difficulties all you have to do is to sit down and begin to listen to God. You begin to speak to Him and you will have an experience. One man described how he had been living a careless and godless life, living for himself to make a name for himself, to make money, living for his family and so on. Then suddenly he came to see how wrong it all was and he began to listen to God. So he wrote a book on his life and told how it was now being lived in relationship to God. And yet it is the literal fact that in that book the Lord Jesus Christ was not even mentioned once. If I understand this Gospel at all, that man is not in relationship to God; he does not know God as Father.

144

I can think of nothing sadder than for men and women to think they are in relationship to God and then find, at the critical moment, that it has all been a delusion. ∾

We must be very plain and clear about this. The times are desperate, they are urgent, and I can think of nothing sadder than for men and women to think they are in relationship to God and then find, at the critical moment, that it has all been a delusion. There are counterfeit experiences; there is an enemy, the devil, who can, according to the apostle Paul, transform himself into a veritable "angel of light" (2 Cor 11:14). He will do anything, he will give any kind of experience as long as he can stand between you and this message of Christ. But here is the statement of the Lord Himself, "I, myself am the way—no man comes unto the Father but by me." Yes, says the apostle Peter, filled with the Holy Spirit, "there is none other name under heaven given among men, whereby we must be saved" (Acts 4:12). "For," says the apostle Paul, speaking of when he went to Corinth, "I determined not to know any thing among you, save Jesus Christ, and him crucified" (1 Cor 2:2). And these men were Jews; they had always believed in God, but what they had come to see was that there is no knowledge of God as Father, no arriving in His presence and spending eternity with Him, except through this Christ of God.

This is the whole essence of the Gospel. Jesus Christ is the only begotten Son of God, and the message is that this eternal Son was "made flesh, and dwelt amongst us" (Jn 1:14). He came as a baby and He dealt with the contradiction of sinners and then He went deliberately to the Cross. He could have avoided it, but He said that He must go through with it otherwise He could not do the work for which He had been sent. So He suffered the agony. We see Him sweating blood and the nails are hammered into His holy flesh, and He died and was buried in a grave. Then He rose again. And I ask, why all that? And there is only one answer, that it was absolutely essential. It is meaningless otherwise. Would God have allowed His only begotten Son to endure all that unless it had been absolutely vital? It was the only way that the Father could bring us to Himself.

Whatever experience you may have, if something happens to you in some mystical sense, whatever it may be, do not rest upon it, do not rely upon it. I am prepared to grant that it may be an agency used by God, but the test of whether it is or not is this, does it lead you to Christ? Does it bring you to see that His coming, His living, His dying, His rising again is the thing that saves you?

That is what He says—"No man cometh unto the Father, but by me." There is but "one mediator between God and men, the man Christ Jesus" (1 Tm 2:5). There is no other way and apart from Him we are lost and undone; we need consider no one else or look in any other direction. Do you desire to know God as your Father? Do you want your prayer to be real? Do you really want to feel that you are in His hands and that the everlasting arms are around you in the moment of crisis and of agony? Very well, look nowhere except to Jesus, to this Christ of God.

All the knowledge that we can ever have is in Him—He is the truth. ∾

And then He amplifies His statement and tells us that He is the way in two vital respects. All the knowledge that we can ever have is in Him—He is the truth. He does not merely talk about it, he does not merely teach or preach, *He Himself is* the truth. The apostle Paul says that in Him "are hid all the treasures of wisdom and knowledge" (Col 2:3). "All right," says someone, "I agree with you that what I really need is to know God and to know Him as my Father, but how can I arrive at that knowledge myself? Must I run to the philosophers or to the various books; must I hope that something mystical will happen to me?" Not at all! You simply look at and come to the Lord Jesus Christ, as you will find Him in these Gospels, and then remember that He said, "He that hath seen me hath seen the Father" (Jn 14:9).

O beloved friend, I know that the concept of God is baffling. The mind boggles at the thought of Him in His infinite greatness and majesty, in all His eternity. So we say, "He is too far away." And, like Philip, we say, "show us the Father." But the question has already been answered. If you want to know what God is like, if you want to know His character, if you want to know truth, look at the Lord Jesus Christ. Look at His love, His mercy, His compassion, His kindness. Look at His readiness to help; He never missed a case of suffering, He always had time to administer His blessing—"He that hath seen me hath seen the Father." God is like that.

Do not think of Him as an enemy, as a great potentate in the distance, as some awful law-giver. He is like Christ. He wants to be like that to you. All the knowledge you have about God is in Christ; you will never have any apart from Him. Also, all you need to know about yourself you will find in Christ and in His teaching. He has shown us very plainly our desperate need. He has come "to seek and to save that which was lost" (Lk 19:10). All you need to know about your relationship to God you will find in Him—*He* is the truth.

But, let me emphasise this again, He is the *truth* and the knowledge of how we can be put right with God. You see, there is only one thing between us and God and that is our sin. It is not our intellect that is defective, it is sin, this barrier that has come in. That is the problem: God is there and we are here. "Why do I not know Him?" asks someone. Because of this barrier. The only way to have it removed is the Lord Jesus Christ. He came in order to be my sin offering; "God was in Christ, reconciling the world unto himself.... He hath made him to be sin for us, who knew no sin; that we might be made the righteousness of God in him" (2 Cor 5:19, 21). There it is—your sin has been laid upon Him, it has been dealt with, it is cleared. Believe it, thank God for it and you will know Him as your Father. Christ "is made unto us wisdom, and righteousness, and sanctification, and redemption" (1 Cor 1:30). "Do you need wisdom?" says Paul to the cultured Greeks. "If you do, go to Christ. He is the wisdom of God, all the truth necessary is in Him." He is the truth.

B*ut, thank God, he is also the way in this respect—He is the life.* ❧

But, thank God, he is also the way in this respect— He is the *life*. Yes, I need the truth and knowledge but I also need the life and power. Do you not know what it is to feel dead, to feel there is no spiritual life in you, to feel that God is far away? How am I to walk through this world; how am I to have communion with God, I feel so weak and frail? And the answer is, He is not only the truth, He is also the life. Again, He does not merely talk about it, He gives it. "In him was life" (Jn 1:4); He has life in Himself; all the fulness of the Godhead dwells in Him bodily (Col 2:9), and any life you need He can give you.

He will quicken and awaken you out of death and sin. He will give you new birth, new life and a new nature. He will come into you and dwell in you and strengthen you. As He said, "I am the vine, ye are the branches" (Jn 15:5). This means that the sap, the nutriment, the power and the life are in Christ; He will spread it to you and express it through you, and the fruit will be seen in you, but the life is in Him. "Without me," He said, "you can do nothing, but in me all things are possible."

Do you feel your will is weak; do you feel your energy is poor? He will come to you, He will strengthen and nerve your feeble will, He will enable you to resist temptation. He will take you above the obstacles and difficulties, he will energise you—that is what He has promised to do. He is life and He will awaken you to life and a knowledge of God and fill you with His power. He will lead you along the journey so that, whatever your circumstances, you will be able to say with the apostle Paul, "I have learned, in whatsoever state I am, therewith to be content. I know both how to be abased, and I know how to abound.... I can do all things through Christ which strengtheneth me" (Phil 4:11-13). A branch that is in the vine and the power of the living Christ is very life itself.

> Ask Him to do this for you; He will introduce you to the Father. ❧

We need it all, do we not?—spiritual life and strength and power and ability to face all that may be awaiting us in this cruel world. It is all offered us freely in Christ. And then, as you face death and the grave, He comes to you and says, "I am the resurrection, and the life" (Jn 11:25). He has conquered even death and the grave; Hades has been despoiled of that which was anticipated. And He will energise you, even through death and the grave and raise you to immortality and incorruption. It is all in Him. "I am the way, the truth, and the life: no man cometh unto the Father, but by me."

Are you in Christ, are you relying upon Him, are you incorporated into Him, do you know God, do you know Him as your Father? If you do not, then apply to Christ immediately. Look on Him, believe on Him, give yourself to Him. Ask Him to do this for you; He will introduce you to the Father. He is the only way whereby you can come to Him.

EIGHT

"Greater Works Than These Shall Ye Do"

And the Lord added to the church daily
such as should be saved.
Acts 2:47b

I T IS MY INTENTION AT THIS POINT to do something
which is perhaps rather different from my usual
method. I propose to give you a general view of the
message which is to be found in the Gospel of John,
chapter 14, from verse 12 more or less to the end of
the chapter. I do so deliberately and resolutely, because
I am anxious to call your attention to the kind of syn-
opsis, which is given here by our Lord and Saviour
Himself, of the results and the effects and the blessings
which follow a true understanding of the meaning of
His death upon the Cross.

We have seen that our Lord, in encouraging His disciples not to be downcast, proceeds to instruct them—
that is always His method of comforting. He never
administers general comfort; His comfort is always

based upon truth, upon doctrine. That is the essential difference between the method of the Christian Gospel and that of all the cults and of psychology. They are all simply concerned to comfort; our Lord has a deeper and a greater object, it is to acquaint us with truth and the comfort is incidental to that. No comfort should be trusted which is not based upon truth. The world is full of many offers of comfort. But we claim that this message alone is true and real and a lasting consolation, because it is based upon the full truth.

> N*o comfort should be trusted which is not based upon truth.* ∾

We have been examining in detail the teaching which our Lord gave His disciples. We have just been considering how He dealt with Thomas' doubts, with the great answer, "I [myself] am the way, the truth, and the life: no man cometh unto the Father, but by me," and how He then has to go on elaborating this, because Philip is in trouble also. "You talk about going to the Father," he says, "but if you could only show us the Father, or if somebody else could, then it would be sufficient." And our Lord has to go over it once more, so He says, "Philip, he that hath seen me hath seen the Father; and how sayest thou then, Shew us the Father? Believest thou not that I am in the Father, and the Father in me? the words that I speak unto you I speak not of myself: but the Father that dwelleth in me, he doeth the works" (Jn 14:9-10). "Do you not realise who I am, Philip?" he says in effect. "Well, if you do not believe what I am saying, believe me for the works—look at the miracles I have performed before you" (v. 11). To believe on the Lord Jesus Christ means a belief in his miracles. You do not explain them psychologically—"Look," He says, "at the works I have performed in your presence, let them testify to you as to who I am, and what I am."

That, then, brings us to the end of verse 11. It is all about the person of the Lord Jesus Christ and His wonderful works. The miracles attest the person, the words spoken attest the person... ah, but the most important work is the work He is going to perform upon the Cross, by dying, by being buried, by rising again and by ascending—the great work of atonement.

If we are not agreed about those points, then what I am going to emphasise now will obviously have no meaning to anyone who is not in agreement. If we are not perfectly clear, I repeat—and it is the very essence of Christian preaching—that Jesus of Nazareth is none other than the only begotten eternal Son of God, come down from heaven, incarnate, in the flesh, here on earth, born miraculously of the Virgin Mary, if we are not clear about these facts, there is no consolation for us in this message.

If we are not clear likewise about the meaning of His death upon the Cross, all the rest is pointless, because it is the very basis of everything. The great apostle Paul, as we have seen, in writing to the church at Corinth, says, "I determined not to know anything among you, save Jesus Christ"—Jesus is the Christ, the Messiah of God—"and him crucified" (1 Cor 2:2). He set Him forth; he placarded Jesus Christ crucified for the sins of men and risen again to justify them. That is the message; that is what our Lord has been saying in verses 1-11.

But that was not enough for the disciples and it is not enough for us. Something more is, in a sense, needed. He had been telling the disciples about their ultimate destination and He told them that He was going to do this work and that He would come back at the end of the age and receive them unto Himself. Yes—but they had to live in the meantime without his physical presence.

"We believe those things," the disciples thought, "but what is going to happen while we are in the world? We still have to go on living, what will happen to us between now and the moment when we come to die, or the day you come back to receive us finally unto yourself?" These are perfectly fair questions. Has the Gospel nothing to offer men and women this side of their arrival in the mansion in the Father's house which is in heaven?

> **What will happen to us between now and the moment when we come to die?** ❧

Now here our Lord answers that question by showing them certain further profound results which will follow from his death and rising again. He tells them a remarkable thing at the end of the chapter. He turns to these men and says that if they had understood these things, far from being sad, they would have rejoiced in His departure! "Ye have heard how I said unto you, I go away, and come again unto you. If ye loved me, ye would rejoice, because I said, I go unto the Father: for my Father is greater than I" (v. 28). It is as if our Lord said to these men, "If you only understood what I am telling you, you know, you would even rejoice because I am going. But you are troubled because of this, because you have not got it clearly, you do not understand it." In other words, He goes on to explain to them how it is that His physical presence with them is not the important thing at all. Indeed, for the reasons I shall remind you of, His physical departure was going to be a good thing for them. He said it again in the sixteenth chapter: "It is expedient for you that I go away: for if I go not away, the Comforter will not come unto you; but if I depart, I will send him unto you" (v. 7). It is *expedient*, a good thing, the best thing that could happen, as it were. "You should rejoice," He says here.

> "*It is expedient for you that I go away: for if I go not away, the Comforter will not come unto you; but if I depart, I will send him unto you.*"

Now let us face this. It is a double message; the first part is this: What is our view of the death of Christ, its meaning and purpose? I wonder whether we are not sometimes guilty, many of us, of exactly the same thing

as these disciples. Have we not often had the feeling
that somehow or another we have missed something
because we have never seen the Lord Jesus Christ with
our own eyes or seen Him in the flesh? Have you not
had that feeling, sometimes, that you wished you had
been living in the days of the disciples? Have you not
said to yourself, "If only I could have been with Him
physically, as Philip and Thomas were, I would not
have found the matter difficult. All would have been
clear." We have the feeling that some of these men had
an advantage over us, but it is terribly foolish to feel
like that. It is a denial of our Lord's own teaching, not
only in this paragraph but elsewhere in these records,
and it is quite wrong.

Let me give you proof of that. This self-same dis-
ciple, Thomas, after the resurrection, you remember,
refused to believe that the Lord had appeared to the
others unless he could see for himself. And the Lord
came again, and when Thomas saw Him he made his
great confession and said, "My Lord and my God."
Yes, but you remember also what Christ said to him:
"Thomas,... blessed are they that have not seen; and
yet have believed" (Jn 20:29). Oh no, physical seeing
is not necessary. Indeed the apostle Paul puts it like this:
"Yea, though we have known Christ after the flesh, yet
now henceforth know we him no more" (2 Cor 5:16).
So it would not help us to see Him with the naked eye.
The people who saw Him in the flesh in that way, who
considered Him an ordinary man, were the people
who said, "Away with him, crucify him." Even these
disciples, who received His teaching as they did, stum-

bled. Let us get rid of that idea once and for ever.

What are our views of His death? Do we regard it as a great tragedy; are we like the disciples? Some people are troubled and disturbed because of it and say, "What a stupid world to crucify this great Teacher! He wasn't old. He would probably have been able to go on for another thirty years giving His noble teaching—what a tragedy that he was cut off at that point!" Others feel that the result of His going at that early age was that He just left us with His teaching and thank God for it! These troubled disciples felt like that somehow.

So let me sum it all up by putting a question. Do we realise what really eventuates from His going to that death? Do we realise the blessings that followed His departure? Do we realise that He went deliberately in order that these things might come to pass? Do we realise—let me put it with reverence—that the best thing that has ever happened in this world for us was that going of the Son of God to the death on Calvary's hill?

> **"I** *never understand why the church calls it* Good *Friday—why not* Bad *Friday, or* Tragic *Friday?"*

I remember a man a few years ago asking me this question: he said, "You know, I never understand why the church calls Good Friday, *Good* Friday—why not *Bad* Friday, or *Tragic* Friday? Surely, it is the worst thing that has happened in the history of mankind and yet you call it Good Friday." Now that is a good way of fixing this question. Do you realise that Good Friday is *Good* Friday and that it is the best day the world has ever known? I am not referring to the men who cried, "Away with Him," or to the men who put Him to death, but I say that what happened on that day is the most wonderful thing that has ever happened—Good Friday, glorious Friday!

This is not a theoretical question, my friends, it is a very practical question. I have been pointing out, as we have considered this great chapter together, that its importance for us is that the greatest need of men and women in the world today is that of a quiet heart. We are troubled, our world is making us so. Daily we hear people telling us how serious things are. What everyone wants is a heart at rest in spite of what is happening around and about us, in spite of all these forebodings of evil. And here is the sovereign remedy, the only remedy. "Believe in me," Christ said; "believe in what I am going to do. Take the right view of life as a pilgrimage to eternity; believe that I am coming back to receive you unto myself. Believe this," He said, "then whatever may happen, your eternity is safe."

"All right," you say, "but what about *now*? How do I get on? What if I have to go through tribulation?" Here is the answer: He comes to meet us exactly where we are. He not only tells us about the ultimate, He prepares us for the present and the immediate future. Let me therefore draw out of this great chapter, from verse 12 onwards, some of the results that followed His going to that death, Resurrection and Ascension.

He not only tells us about the ultimate, He prepares us for the present and the immediate future. ∾

There are the things He tells us: the first is that His
going does not mean that His work will stop; rather,
that it will increase. "Verily, verily I say unto you, He
that believeth on me, the works that I do shall he do
also; and greater works than these shall he do; because
I go unto my Father" (v. 12). What a marvellous statement! And, you see, it is relevant to the disciples.
There they were, a group of men who had certain
ideas about Him. They said that He was wonderful,
that His teaching was incomparable, that He was a
perfect leader. They were looking forward to great
days that were coming, when suddenly He said, "I am
going." And they said, "If He is going, that means an
end to His work. If He is going out of the world how
can it be carried on?" And that was His answer—
"greater works than these shall he do, because I go
unto my Father."

Now He was not referring to physical miracles—no
greater physical miracles were worked by the apostles
than were worked by Christ Himself. He was referring
to something qualitative. What He meant was that He
had referred to His physical miracles in attesting His
own authority, but that those who believed in Him
were going to do "greater things"—the spiritual miracles which followed Pentecost, which are recorded in
the Acts of the Apostles and in the subsequent history
of the Christian Church. Have you ever thought of

that? We tend to misunderstand the death of Christ at this point and the misunderstanding is always due to the same reason, that we are somehow not clear about His person or His death. You see, if we think of Him only as man—as the disciples did at that point—we will not understand it. If we are only interested in His teaching we will not understand it. But the moment we begin to understand the meaning of His death, then the whole situation becomes entirely changed.

Let me put it like this. There is an incident that is recorded in John 12, when certain Greeks came, desiring to have an interview with Him. The message was passed on to Him but He did not see them and, in that connection, He made this momentous and profound statement: "I," He said, "if I be lifted up from the earth, will draw all men unto me" (Jn 12:32). In a sense, while He was still here on earth as a human teacher, He was nothing but the Jewish Messiah and misunderstood at that. "I cannot see the Greeks now," He said in effect, "there is no point in it; but when I die, I become the Saviour of the world, the Saviour of mankind."

> While he was still here on earth as a human teacher, he was nothing but the Jewish Messiah and misunderstood at that.... His real work of saving mankind happens after the Cross. ❧

And that, in a way, is the very thing He is saying here. I again say it, with reverence and carefully, His real work of saving mankind happens after the Cross.

He talked about it but the disciples did not understand it. He constantly told them about His death and resurrection, but they did not grasp it. It was only afterwards, as they looked back from Pentecost, when they were filled with the Holy Spirit, that they saw it. It is on Calvary's hill that the fountain for sin and uncleanness is opened. It is by bearing the sins of mankind in His body on the tree that He becomes the Saviour of the world. The work must be done first and then it can be released. If you like, it is there that the great source is tapped and opened and from there the stream will pour forth and make fruitful the whole world of men and women.

And, of course, history confirms this. Take the accounts of the Gospels. Here was this incomparable preacher, this wonderful teacher, this miracle worker, and yet He attracted but few followers to Himself. He was rejected and forsaken even by His own intimate circle of followers and He went to a violent death upon the Cross, which made the scoffers say He was a failure. And then you see a man like Simon Peter—of everybody!—the impulsive, unreliable Peter, preaching one sermon at Jerusalem and three thousand people were converted and saved. Oh yes, "Greater works than these shall he do; because I go unto my Father."

The Cross has to happen first, there is the essential preliminary, the matter without which there is no salvation. It must be done first and then the power of the Holy Spirit comes to apply it. His going does not mean the end of the work; it means, and will mean, the continuing and the carrying on of the work in a still greater, and in a still more wonderful manner. There I see them crowding into the kingdom on the day of Pentecost, three thousand of them. Then I see Peter, called to the Gentiles at Caesarea, and the doorway to the Gentiles is opened, and I see them streaming in. And the Gospel is preached throughout the whole world—"greater works than these shall he do"—it is the death of Christ upon the Cross that really gives to us and brings to us these great and glorious and wondrous blessings from God.

Then the second point is this: His help in prayer. "Whatsoever ye shall ask in my name, that will I do, that the Father may be glorified in the Son. If ye shall ask any thing in my name, I will do it" (Jn 14:13-14). What a long time we could spend on these verses! But let me say this in summarising them. You see the position? Here are these men, crestfallen. They say, "In trouble we always turn to Him, and now He is going; what can we do? He takes the decisions and now we will not have Him to refer to." And His reply is, "Foolish men; you can pray to me. I will be there with the Father; I will be the great high priest to whom your prayers will come. I will be with you in these matters and when you pray in my name I will do it."

It is a message which comes to us at this present time. If you are clear about Him, His person and work and what He has done, if you know your sins are forgiven, if you know you are a Christian, a child of God, then I say to you that He tells you here to go to Him, whatever your need. Whatever your position, go to Him in confidence and He will be with you, He will be there. "Speak to me," He says. "I am here and I will present your petition to the Father." What a wonderful promise to men and women who may have to face things too terrible even to imagine. Are you preparing for things like that? Cannot you see that a time may come in your life when you will be so desperate that nobody will be able to help you and you will be left alone? What do you do? Child of God, speak to Him, He is there. Christ tells you he is going in order that such a confidence may be possible. He has died for you; He has made you a child of God and you can have the confidence of a child. You can go to God, knowing He is your Father, and pray in the name of Christ. He promises to deal with your petition. I cannot imagine anything more glorious or wonderful than that.

> H*e has made you a child of God and you can have the confidence of a child.* ༄

The next thing He tells them is that His departure does not even mean that His work in them, and for them, will come to an end, because He gives them the great promise of the Holy Spirit. "I will pray the Father, and he shall give you another Comforter [another Advocate], that he may abide with you for ever; Even the Spirit of truth; whom the world cannot receive, because it seeth him not, neither knoweth him; but ye know him; for he dwelleth with you, and shall be in you" (vv. 16-17). This again is amazing and

astounding; do you see what it means? These men
turned to one another and, in effect, said, "Well now,
if He is going to leave us, we will have nobody to teach
us. We have had all this wonderful teaching for three
years, but, alas, it is suddenly coming to an end, we
cannot remember all that He said and we cannot go
on. What will happen to us?"

"Silence," says Christ; "I am going to send the Holy
Spirit to you and He will not only be with you, He will
be in you. Do you know," He said to them, "it is
going to be a good thing for you. I am a teacher outside you, but I will send a teacher who will be inside
you. He will recall to you everything that I have ever
said. He will lead you into further truth and explain it
to you. You will have within you a source of knowledge that will amaze and astound you." That is why
He said that it was expedient for them that He should
go away. The Holy Spirit enters into the believer and
he has a teacher within him; he is given understanding.

> The Holy Spirit enters into the
> believer and he has a teacher within
> him; he is given understanding. ∾

This was the great theme of the apostle Paul. He, of
all men, with his gigantic mind and intellect, it was he
who said, "The wise men of the world cannot understand this preaching of the Cross and of the blood, it is
folly to them." Of course, it is because they are trying
with their natural finite minds to understand, and no
man can do it. But "the Spirit searcheth all things, yea

the deep things of God." The Spirit we have received is "not the spirit of the world, but the spirit which is of God; that we might know the things that are freely given to us of God" (1 Cor 2:8, 12). Look at these stumbling disciples, uncertain of the person, stumbling at the fact of His death, not understanding the Resurrection—O what hopeless men they are, and how dejected! Then look at them in the Acts of the Apostles expounding the Scriptures, understanding Him, understanding the meaning of His death and the atonement; preaching, writing, teaching, filled with a new understanding. It is the unction and anointing of the Holy Spirit; He promised it and it happened.

*A**dmit your bankruptcy and failure.
Ask Him for the unction of the
Holy Spirit and you will have it.* ❧

And you, if you do not understand these things, you have but to take Him at His word and believe on Him and ask Him for the Holy Spirit and He will give Him to you. Admit your bankruptcy and failure. Ask Him for the unction of the Holy Spirit and you will have it, and you will begin to understand and to know the things that have baffled you hitherto—what a wonderful promise! He will enable you to understand the course of history. You will no longer be surprised at the world or by wars and rumours of wars. You will see the unfolding of God's plan of the age; with the unction and anointing of the Holy Spirit you will see the end. Do you understand? Are you running from teacher to teacher, and from book to book? Here is everything you need but you need the presence of the Holy Spirit within you to understand it.

And lastly, He says that His going away will actually mean that He will be with them in a more real sense than he has ever been before. "I will not leave you comfortless,"—I will not leave you orphans— "I will come to you. Yet a little while, and the world seeth me no more; but ye see me: because I live, ye shall live also" (vv. 18-19). And then come the sublime and astounding words that follow, where He says that He Himself, and the Father, will come and dwell and take up their abode within the life of these believers (v. 23). "If you really understood these things," said Christ, "you would rejoice when I say I am going. Why?—for this reason; I am going physically and in the body but it just means that I will come back and live within you, not only by your side. I am going to dwell *in* you."

Amazing doctrine, baffling to the understanding and yet true—"I live," says Paul, "yet not I, but Christ liveth in me" (Gal 2:20). Yes, says Christ, "Behold, I stand at the door, and knock"—I want to come in. "If any man hear my voice, and open the door, I will come in to him, and will sup with him, and he with me" (Rv 3:20). "Oh do not be troubled by my announcement of my departure," He says to the disciples who are not clear about these things; "it does not mean I am going from you; I am coming back and will live within you." This is the supreme offer, the supreme blessing of the Christian Gospel, that it tells us that if we but believe these things, and commit ourselves to them, then God will come and dwell within us, Christ will take up His abode in our hearts. So that whatever may happen to us, whatever the world may do unto us, whatever may be taken from us, whatever calamity may overwhelm us, He will always remain. He says He will abide for ever and ever. In the flesh He came and He went, but now He comes spiritually and dwells within us.

> *I*n the flesh He came and He went, *but now He comes spiritually and dwells within us.* ❧

Now, I do not know how you feel, but as I finished reading and studying this chapter and preparing this message, I said to myself that from now on, I shall pray that prayer that the great and saintly Hudson Taylor[1] prayed every day of his life. When Hudson Taylor died, they found in his Bible a kind of bookmark, just a sheet of paper. As he read his Bible, so he moved the paper every day. It is a prayer; here it is and it seems to me to be the most vital thing we can ever pray:

Lord Jesus make Thyself to me,
A living bright reality,
More present to faith's vision keen
Than any outward object seen;
More near, more intimately nigh
Than e'en the sweetest earthly tie.

If only we know for certain that the Christ of God is in us; if only we can say with Paul, "Christ liveth in

---

1. The founder of the China Inland Mission, now the Overseas Missionary Fellowship.

me," then we will be able to say with Paul that nothing that may happen to us can in any way "separate us from the love of God, which is in Christ Jesus our Lord" (Rom 8:39). We not only believe things about Him, we not only believe on Him, we are to *know* Him and to experience Him and His eternal wondrous life being lived out in us. It is wrong, it is unscriptural, it is even sinful to stop at anything less than that. He not only died that we might be forgiven; He died in order that He might come and live in us.

Oh make certain that He dwells in you, for if He does, your heart will not be troubled, neither will it be afraid.